The Divorce

Harper Golin

Copyright © 2024 by Harper Golin

All rights reserved.

No portion of this book may be reproduced in any form without written permission from the publisher or author, except as permitted by U.S. copyright law.

contents

1: News	1
2: Shell	13
3: Off	28
4: Yearn	42
5: Him	53
6: Taste	65
7: Ring	76
8: Date	86
9: Alone	102
10: Decisions	116
11: Curse	129
12: Attract	141
13: Repel	153

14: Stranger	165
15: Cliché	178
16: Fallen	189
17: Boyfriend	200
18: Years	210
19: Photographs	220
20: Tension	230
21: Leave	241
22: Blood	255
23: Surprise	270
24: Lust	287
25: Sick	300

1: News

"Who's right, who's wrong Who really cares? The fault, the blame, the pain's still there I'm here alone inside of this broken home"

~.~.~

The flight was long and the jet lag was killing me.

On hearing my phone buzz, I answered with a sigh, "Where are you, Gary?"

"Shh! Someone will hear you!" He shot back, "Look to your right. Blue cap, shades, and a mask" I turned to find a familiar figure in the distance and rushed towards him immediately.

"It's so good to see you!" Just as I was about to hug him, he pushed me by my shoulders. "Not here, in the car" He warned.

I rolled my eyes, "Celebrities"

"You don't need to remind me of how lucky you are" His smirk was so evident even though he was wearing a mask. As cocky as always.

Gary helped me with the luggage and we finally drove out of the airport. Now, he had taken off all his facial accessories and I noticed the silver piercing in his ear. His dirty blonde hair was such a mess that I began wondering how often he showered.

"Tania got this for me" He grinned and tapped the earing, "I think it's her way of asking— no ordering, me to marry her"

"That's cute" I chuckled.

Gary had been dating Tania for over a year now and honestly, I was shocked that he could be in a committed relationship with someone.

He was so wild, and talented.

At thirty, Gary Wilson was extremely popular worldwide but he never wanted to keep a bodyguard. Instead, he liked playing hide and seek with the paparazzi. He was in every soccer magazine and sports commercial. Gary, being the star that he was, had played in the World Cup at just nineteen. Ever since then, he has been one of the most celebrated players on the planet. I was so proud and happy for him, even my parents were.

I remembered Dad having second thoughts about his entire soccer ordeal.

When Gary was fourteen, he caused so many problems at the boarding school that Dad was forced to talk to him personally. He asked Gary why his grades had dropped below average, he mustered enough courage to tell Dad that he was trying to qualify for the national football team.

Dad never opposed his dream, a part of him even felt relieved that Gary at least knew what he wanted. Leonardo Xander had let the teenager join clubs and go for practice even though he never believed that Gary would qualify.

But he did, and that shocked all of us.

For the first time, Gary had sincerely done something in his life.

On the day when Dad lectured Gary, I was in his study— curiously watching him work and feeling inspired. Dad never complained when I came around and climbed onto his lap. He would be more than willing because he always said that I paid attention to his work instead of getting distracted like Mom.

It was only because I didn't want to disturb him. Ever since I was little, people have been telling me that I was too proper.

I still try to be.

Mom had once remarked while she was drunk after a party, "I don't know how you do it sweetheart, and I love you so, so much for it.

You're the sweetest little angel I've ever known, and I want you to stay that way" She hugged and kissed me while feeling all emotional.

"Please, don't turn out like me or your father"

Mom would always tell me that.

I was very glad that I could easily remember every little detail about my life in the twenty-two years that I had lived. Dad said that it was a gift because if he were to remember all the nuisances that Mom had caused him, he'd probably go insane.

I missed them. Especially the fights.

It often started with something silly, till the entire atmosphere flared up and I would be forced to resign to my room. But probably an hour into the fight, I'd walk back downstairs and find them making out like teenagers on the kitchen counter.

One time I nearly walked in on them.

I dreaded that memory too much.

The good thing— even though I'm still confused about whether it's actually good— is that my parents don't shy away from anything.

They have given me the thorough birds and the bees talk, or even a high degree of it. I had no idea how Dad could explain certain things with a straight face. He was even proud that he could get Mom to moan his name every day.

Even though the walls in my room were mostly soundproof, I could very much hear my mom's happy screams if she tried hard.

They were disgusting.

But their daily rendezvous gave me another reason to go over to Annie's place as an excuse to study. She was always so fun and supportive, probably the closest I had to a best friend. Even Arthur would be with her because she helped both of us study. After all, Annie was a college professor. She loved teaching.

I loved them like my own siblings because we had grown up together, literally. Uncle Jeff and Aunt Leana would drop Arthur and Annie off at our place when they had places to go to. Mom and Dad would do the same with me sometimes, and I would always look forward to spending the day with them.

Arthur was completely like a brother to me, he had even claimed it himself— I'm his sister from another mother. On many occasions, he had specifically mentioned that he would like to replace Annie with me. She would say the same.

They were so chaotic and I would end up being the one to break the ice between them.

Maybe it was because I didn't want to lose either Annie or Arthur.

They were part of the handful of people who actually cared about me.

Gary was just as close to me as Arthur, even though he and Annie talked shit about each other all the time. I loved Gary's honesty more than anything. He never held back while telling me about something and I knew that I could trust him. Especially, because Dad trusted him.

At least, Dad trusted him to the extent of letting him pick me up from the airport. That was a big leap.

My father has never let me get close to guys. Never.

When I was younger, Dad made it a point to make Jay pick me up from school in a black SUV. Mom said that he purposefully did it to scare the boys so that they kept away from me, and boy they did.

Hence making my social life a fucking mess.

I had absolutely no friends in school.

The only people he trusted to get close to me were Arthur, Annie, Gary, and Danny.

He trusted Danny too much but I didn't.

Danny was a mystery of his own.

That man was intimidating beyond words.

"Are you paying attention, nerd?" Gary glared at me.

"Huh?"

"I've been asking how you have been for the past five minutes"

"Oh, I... I'm fine..."

"Lucy... I know that the divorce has been hard on you, and I know that you're not going to tell anyone because you're too much of a cinnamon roll"

I squeezed the phone in my hands.

Yes, it was hard.

It was the hardest news that I've ever had to swallow.

A year after I left for college, Mom phoned me. She had been crying bitterly and she said that Dad wanted a divorce.

None of it made sense.

They had so much history together.

Mom loved him so much. She never hesitated to say it to his face.

Sometimes I thought that my father was a terrible person because he never confessed.

He never once did anything romantic for her wholeheartedly.

He never once tried.

I was so mad at everything. At them. But I couldn't say anything.

By the time I was nineteen, their divorce was done.

Dad, as usual, continued working at Xander Corp and Mom moved back to her old apartment. At least she had her art studio.

They both went on with their lives like nothing happened.

Like they hadn't looked at each other in a lovesick way. Like they hadn't openly flirted in front of me. Like they hadn't touched or kissed like eternal lovers.

Dad used to be so proud of everything. He was especially proud of having the most beautiful woman on Earth as his wife— his exact words.

Yet, he threw it all away.

At first, I thought that Dad had brought up the divorce during one of their countless arguments.

But when I talked to him, he said that he was very serious about the decision.

"Are you... Um... Seeing someone else then?" I remembered asking him. I hated the question myself.

"No Cupcake," He had sighed over the phone, "It's either your mother or it's nobody"

Then why?!

I wanted to scream at him and shove him away for all the terrible things he had done to her.

My mom was incredible.

She put up with his bullshit better than anyone, and she never complained.

A part of me hated that attribute about her because I had inherited it.

The inability to complain. A curse that forced you to put others first.

"I hope you are" Gary sighed and pulled over in front of my place. "I have a photoshoot in half an hour, so I can't come inside. Say hi to my godfather for me" He winked before driving away.

I laughed and shook my head. Gary loved mocking Dad by calling him that.

The guard helped carry my luggage as we walked towards the lawn. There, in all his glory, I saw Dad doze off at the kitchen table. He was holding a cup of coffee but his eyes were long closed and his hair was disheveled.

I mean, who could blame my mom for loving him so selflessly?

The man was gorgeous even in his late fifties.

If I were to overlook his shortcomings, there were many things that I loved about Dad. First and foremost, his patience. Mom said that he never had an ounce of it in the beginning but over the years he had changed a lot.

"It's because I deal with two toddlers every day" Dad had whispered while nuzzling against Mom's stomach as he fell asleep on her lap. He always did that.

Moreover, Dad was hardworking. He loved his company like a second child and he spent so much time making it better. I wish he'd retire and rest but he always said that he was waiting for the day I take over.

The secret to his beauty, Mom said, was that he worked out often. His health wasn't bad. It was above average than most men his age and he kept it that way. Dad had quit alcohol long back and never ate junk food. But I despised it when he smoked cigarettes.

Kelly, the housekeeper he had hired after Lara, was a tiny bit older than me. But boy, did she have her eyes on my Dad. Both Mom and

I knew her intentions, and Mom even threatened to fire her once because she caught Kelly trying to touch Dad's hand.

Personally, I didn't think that Dad cared.

He was always so indifferent and professional with his workers. I think he had the same attitude with everyone.

Only Mom and I have ever made him laugh and we held it as a huge achievement.

Nobody would ever be able to get close to him besides us.

Nobody.

Not even the thirsty twenty-something booby woman who was busy watching my dad like a hawk.

I tiptoed towards him and Kelly spotted me, I placed my finger on my lips asking her to be quiet. Slowly, I wrapped my arms around Dad's and hugged him from behind while nuzzling into the crook of his neck. His stubble was as scratchy as always. Mom used to love it.

"Chelsea?" He whispered, waking up.

I was stunned to hear him say Mom's name.

"It's me Dad" I chuckled and kissed his cheek.

Dad turned to look at me. He smiled and caressed my face but I saw a certain disappointment in his eyes. Was he really sad over the fact that it was me instead of Mom?

"Welcome home Cupcake. How was the flight?"

"It was okay" I lied, just like always. "Gary had a shoot so he left after dropping me off. I thought you were going to pick me up?"

"I had a meeting till 1.30 in the morning... After that, I was waiting for your flight but it became terribly delayed so I guess I couldn't sleep" His voice sounded tired, and even his eyes looked different.

Like he had lost the light in them.

Of course, he had.

He pushed her away.

Almost on instinct, I turned around thinking that Mom would walk over to us with a bright grin on her face, but it was just the wind.

The house was not the same without her.

I hated it.

Last Edited: 10/11/23Lyrics: Broken Home by 5 Seconds of Summer

2: SHELL

"It's beautiful, it's bittersweet You're like a broken home to me I take a shot of memories and black out like an empty street"

~.~.~

Dad and I took a long nap in our rooms because I was terribly jet-lagged while he... He looked like life had been sucked out of him.

I woke up in the evening and found the missed calls in my phone left by Jay. He was usually fun to be around and that was the only reason I had agreed when Dad sent him to accompany me in college.

He would always stay around me like a bodyguard 'cause Dad strictly prohibited boys and other forms of 'bad influence'.

Jay was cool though, he always found ways to turn the mood and sometimes Mathew— Dad's long-lasting PA— visited us to make sure that I was doing alright. Secretly, I knew that Mathew was coming around just to meet Jay. After all, they were happily married now.

The both of us stayed in separate rooms at a posh apartment all through college and that cut my chances of making friends completely. I was pretty sure that the rest of the kids thought that I was dating Jay. I never even got a chance to correct the misunderstandings.

All thanks to Dad.

At least Mom would listen to my watered-down complaints. After the divorce, she began calling me a lot more. Now that my parents weren't in each other's company, they wanted my affection. I honestly felt sorry for them.

After texting Jay and attaching a picture of my bedroom to confirm that I was safe at home, he let me go without another text message.

Alvarez still cooked for us and he always knew what I loved to eat. A very delicious fruit cake was waiting for me in the kitchen. I turned to Alvarez after eating, "When Dad wakes up, tell him that I'm with Mom"

He nodded and I took my car from the garage. The silver BMW was something that Dad gifted me for my graduation. I loved driving it around whenever I was home.

I parked outside Mom's apartment and hurried up the stairs. After frantically knocking, she opened the door beaming, "Sweetheart!"

She squealed and pulled me in the biggest bear hug ever, "I missed you so much!"

"I missed you too Mom" I laughed.

"The room is as messy as always huh?" I chuckled while stepping inside. There were buckets of paint everywhere and a canvas was fixed in the middle of the room.

"Is this your new one?"

"Yep!" She put down her paintbrush and stood by me, "It has a long way to go"

"It's beautiful Mom" I kissed her cheek before lying down on the bed.

"Have you eaten yet?" She asked.

"Yeah, Alvarez made a really good cake"

"Don't make me drool" She sighed and continued painting again.

I told her that I was done with my internship and that I'd start working at Xander Corp now. Dad had already offered to give me a directorial post but I had denied him. I wanted to start from the bottom and make my way up. When I was ready to take over his second child, he would know. But now I needed experience.

"You're such a beautiful successful girl, Lucy" Mom smiled at me.

Unlike Dad, who always made sure that I wasn't spoiled, Mom was different. It felt like she was doing it on purpose. She knew how much Dad had always kept me restricted, yet he provided me with everything. She told me that it was his way of showering love but I didn't like it.

But of course, I never complained.

I was pathetic.

"Did you meet any pretty guys?"

"Uhm..." I blushed and told her about the few guys that I had admired from afar.

"Lucy" She rolled her eyes, "You should have talked to them"

"Yeah, and let Dad kill them? No thank you"

Mom scowled at the mention of his name, "You're a grown woman. That asshole can't control you anymore"

I was shocked to hear such words from her. A second after she said it, she looked guilty herself, "I'm sorry... I- I shouldn't say such things about your father in front of you" Her eyes were fixed on the painting. She's never reacted that way before.

"Mom, are you okay?"

"I just got carried away" She faked a smile, "Would you like to go out to dinner? Just a mom and daughter outing? No men involved"

"Okay" I agreed.

***

When I returned home, Dad was having dinner in the kitchen while Kelly was chatting away. He wasn't even paying attention to anything. He looked so lost.

"Dad?"

"Ah, you're back" He smiled, "Sit down. Tell me everything you were up to. And Kelly, you can lock up"

I was glad for the last part. It felt so good to just sit next to him and rant away about my boring college life and internship. I didn't think that Dad was listening though, he was simply watching me.

Dad was smiling, feeling content that his Cupcake was back.

"I could officially give you a tour tomorrow," He said when I talked about Xander Corp.

"Dad, I know every nook and crevice there" I chuckled, remembering all the times that I had considered the large building as my playground. Jay often took me there after school or I would end up at Mom's studio.

I was personally glad that Mom and Dad didn't get me a nanny. They felt completely responsible when it came to me and considering how protective Dad could get, he didn't want to let a stranger into my life.

But since I was a quiet curious kid, I enjoyed both workplaces.

"You may know the places, Cupcake, but you don't know what we do in each corner. I'll show you everything tomorrow" He replied.

After a long pause, Dad asked me something strange, "How was... Your evening? What did Chelsea say?"

"Why do you wanna know?" I replied innocently.

Dad cleared his throat, "Did she tell you who she was seeing?"

My jaw dropped.

"What?"

"Hmm... I thought she told you"

"She didn't mention anything..."

An awkward silence.

"Well, Lucy. You have to wake up early tomorrow. I have a meeting at 9, I'll show you around before that and you can start working whenever you like. I'll tell Mathew to keep your office ready"

"But he's in UK with Jay..."

"It's about time those slackers came back" Dad muttered and took out his phone.

***

The door flung open revealing Arthur's goofy grin.

"Mom said that you'd be here. Welcome back, Lucy!" He squeezed the life out of me.

"Let the girl live!" Annie smacked his arm and he pouted at her.

We were all nestled on her bed, watching movies just the way we used to. Arthur dug his hand into the bowl of popcorn and stuffed it in his mouth.

"So, what are your plans now?"

"I'll start working for Dad by Monday. Then, I guess I'll just settle here. I missed home a lot"

"Damn, a few of my friends are dying to get into your Dad's company. It's like the best in the world, even my dad asked me to go for it once, but of course, I prefer science" Arthur sighed, it was as though he was confessing his love for someone.

"Well, I think you're overqualified to be working already. I mean, girl, you passed out from Yale. That's a very big deal"

I blushed, "You don't have to keep saying it"

"Of course I'll say it" Annie smirked, "It's incredible Lucy, be proud of it!"

I hummed.

"So, any hot guys yet?" Arthur asked while holding back his laugh. Even Annie squealed when he brought it up, "Sure, like the great Leonardo Xander will let them live" I got deja vu

"It's pathetic how you haven't even kissed a guy"

"I have kissed a guy" I muttered.

But after that, he kept a 500-mile distance from me.

"What?!"

Both Arthur and Annie yelled at the same time.

"I kissed Danny"

"You were a baby" Arthur scoffed, "That doesn't count"

I pursed my lips.

I wish I could tell them about the second time we kissed.

To put it more correctly, he had kissed me.

It was during one of Gary's games in Turkey and my parents had surprisingly taken me to watch it (they rarely did). My sixteen-year-old self was too overwhelmed by the crowd. I was a sick introvert and I hated it. Claustrophobia had hit me badly.

Danny was doing his residency at that time. He had graduated from a reputed medical school and my Dad allowed him to take me away from the crowd.

Since we were VIPs, Danny took me to the hotel room where his brother was staying. We were sitting on the bed, with his arm around me to calm me down.

~~~

"You're fine, Lucy"

His hands were running up and down my shoulders, it felt so good to be comforted like this. So good.

"Danny... Tell me when he scores a goal"

Danny chuckled and I looked up at him. He was 26, far too old to be comforting a teenager like this but he didn't mind. I'm glad he didn't.

In my entire lifetime, we might have had six meaningful conversations. They were numbered. But I liked that Danny rarely talked to anyone except my Dad.

Whenever I saw him at parties, he always seemed to have his life in his fist. He knew what he wanted. He knew how to work for it. He knew how it was all going to go.

Dad would often tell me that Danny was a wonderful boy. It was so rare for him to praise someone that way. Danny was very lucky.

"Look! He scored," Danny grinned at the TV and I took a peek as well. Not at the TV, but at Danny's face.

Fine golden brown hair was dusted on his chin and under his nose but it couldn't be called a stubble yet. He looked boyish, like the guys in my class. But unlike them, he wasn't spreading false rumors about me.

I was sixteen.

I doubted if there were virgins in my class and here I was, without a first kiss.

But Danny had kissed me once, by accident though. Gary told me about it while he was drunk one time.

It certainly wouldn't hurt to reach out and peck his cheek.

It was just his cheek.

There was nothing wrong with it. I had done it multiple times when I was younger.

But it felt different now.

Maybe, just maybe, I might start coming out of my shell with this.

My hand reached up to hold the side of his face. Danny froze. He was completely petrified.

When I brushed my lips against his cheek, I felt his arm squeeze my shoulder tighter. He was strong, a bit too strong.

"Thanks for coming with me here" I whispered, trying to hold back my blush but I couldn't.

His eyes flickered down to mine, they were often a mild brown shade but now they were black. Pitch black.

He wasn't smiling. His eyes were holding me steady. They looked deep and... Dangerous?

I had never felt intimidated by him before. At least not to this extent.

Danny caressed my cheek with his knuckles.

"Lucy..."

I didn't recognize the hoarseness in his voice.

I didn't even recognize the guy I just kissed.

"Don't do that"

There was nothing friendly about his tone. It was cold like metal. And honestly, he was scaring me. I tried pulling away but his grip was too strong.

Danny slowly moved his face toward me.

My heart was beating wildly against my chest.

I thought I'd die when his nose touched mine.

I couldn't breathe because of our proximity.

His eyes were so damn deep. I was beginning to forget the entirety of my surroundings.

"Don't fucking do that" He growled.

I couldn't even process it because his lips were on mine.

The hand around my shoulder, moved down, pulling me by the waist.

I couldn't react to anything.

His tongue invaded me wholly.

And I let him.

My body felt so completely limp that the only thing I could do was place my hand against his chest.

A part of me was relieved that his heart was thumping just as madly.

He was rough.

So rough.

He bit my lips, sliding his tongue against mine, our teeth bumping because I was such an inexperienced kisser.

How could a person even be this skilled?

Was this even right?

What if Mom and Dad catch us in the act?

He was ten years older than me for fucks sake!

But Dad was clearly 13 years older than Mom... They seem to be doing alright.

Still, he was twenty-six and I was still a damn minor.

Danny could get arrested for this.

I couldn't even shake the ominous feeling that had settled on me.

But I liked it.

I liked the way he was so thirsty for me.

Desperate.

It was like Danny had been starved for a lifetime.

I squeezed his well-pressed shirt, crinkling it, and found myself unconsciously moaning against his lips.

But this was all rushed!

My mind was racing too fast.

"Danny?" I heard a loud knock on the door.

Thank you, Dad!

Danny pulled back and stared at me in horror. It felt like he had realized his actions now.

Even I was left speechless.

What just happened?

I certainly didn't want my parents to catch me like this.

In the blink of an eye, I laid down and pulled the sheets over me. Danny got off the bed, fixed his clothes, and opened the door.

"Is she okay?" Dad asked, his voice laced with concern.

I was not okay.

"Yes... Uh... She fell asleep..." Danny replied seeing that I was under the blankets.

"Come on downstairs. We should let her sleep" Dad told him.

They left after closing the door.

Danny's expression revealed that the kiss was terrible. The worst in his life.

But he was good.

So very good.

I wondered if all kisses felt like this— hot and wet, and so very confusing.

Somehow the experience had pushed me farther into my shell.

Last Edited: 13/11/23Lyrics: Beautiful Mistakes by Maroon 5

3: OFF

"Kiss and Crawl right back

Under the covers

Down for another

Hour in the bed

Now I'm here instead"

~-~-~

It had been a week since I came home and I was starting to absolutely hate it.

Dad was off.

He was off on so many levels.

And I couldn't even talk to Mom as she was extremely infuriated at him.

I swear that they used to fight like Neanderthals and made up for it on sexual terms but this... This was terrible. Mom used to get mad at him, sure, but not to this level. She was practically spitting fire at every mention of his name.

The divorce was unexpected for everyone. Literally everyone.

I remembered what Jay had once told me about it, "I've never seen two people who can't communicate— well, like people— yet stay so emotionally drawn to each other"

He was right. Leonardo and Chelsea Xander had a rough start.

I had heard it from Lara herself when I was young, but when Dad succumbed to the freeze, he became more... Human...

I knew all about his shitty childhood. Mom had told me not to hurt him because we were all that he had, even though he seemed to take things for granted. I knew all about his misfortune.

But I could bet on my silver BMW that somewhere in Dad's heart, he loved Mom.

He loved her just as much as myself.

He has always cared for her with his actions more than his words. Dad might be rude but if Mom ever needed him by her side, he would always be there.

They were a match made in hell and heaven.

"Did anything else happen at work, hmm?" She smiled and rested her chin on her fist. Even at 45, Mom was gorgeous. It was something that even Dad never hesitated to admit.

"No. It was boring, I told you. I did expect my first day to be more fun actually..."

Mom grunted, "There's nothing fun about that stupid blue building"

"Why are you and Dad behaving like literal zombies?"

"Your dad," She scoffed, "He's always been a zombie. Dead on the inside, every damn time"

That was it.

My last thread of patience had snapped.

"Why are you behaving like this? I don't understand. You've been roasting Dad ever since I got here and I'm not trying to protect him but I deserve to know, Mom. Did something else happen?"

My mom looked away, staring at her tablet. There was a pained frown on her face.

"Nothing happened" She mumbled.

"Mom, don't do that... You can't lie to me"

"I promise that there's nothing wrong, sweetheart" She mustered another smile.

I sighed, "Dad said that you're seeing someone"

She froze and looked up, "What else did he say?"

"He asked if I knew the guy... Are you really talking shit about Dad because of your new relationship?"

"There is no new guy" Mom muttered and stared back at the tablet. That thing was getting on my nerves.

"He wouldn't stop interfering with me, so I had to lie"

My eyes widened like saucers, "He interfered?"

"He came to meet me, Lucy. Looking as stuck up as always"

"And?" I leaned towards her in curiosity.

"Aren't you the Pandora's box? We talked. He left. That's it"

"Talked?" I chuckled, "You guys don't talk. You either fight it out or kiss it out or... I don't even want to go there" I pretended to puke.

"You need to sleep" Mom glared, color rushing to her cheeks.

"Hold on, what I predicted just now, is it true?"

"Sleep, Lucy!" She snapped and walked over to the balcony to complete her work.

[~ Chelsea's POV ~]

I hated it when she asked those questions.

But I couldn't blame her. After all, Lucy got her words from him. That bastard who had the audacity to touch me after three years of being divorced.

~~~

A knock on the door.

While getting up to answer it, I never predicted it would be him of all people.

The asshole who bit my heart and left me bleeding.

The one guy who left me feeling hot every night for three years straight.

He was standing before me in all of his charismatic glory.

Navy blue suit, white shirt, well-defined chest, gray stubble, messy and peppered hair, tired pale green eyes, and such a beautiful face. Leo was too much of the perfect dilf.

Seeing him in person for the first time in 3 years was daunting.

Especially because he managed to look like a disheveled meal.

A part of me wanted to drop to my knees and take him right away, but the wiser part of me wanted to grab the kitchen knife and stab his chest a hundred times.

The wound he left could never be compared to any other pain.

His eyes— fuck his eyes— they roamed up and down my body. The way he always devoured me with just his fucking eyes was pathetic. His tongue grazed his lower lip.

Oh my god.

I haven't had sex in three years and this man had the audacity of knocking on my door like he's dinner.

"Fuck"

That's the first thing that rolls out of his mouth as he takes a deep breath while analyzing my features. Always, I'm under his scrutiny.

"You're not wearing anything under that nightdress, are you?"

I certainly was not expecting that.

And my first instinct was to slam the door in his face.

To tell him to fuck off.

The very same way he had filed for a divorce.

I didn't know what I had done wrong at the time.

I tried everything— every fucking thing— to meet the standards of his royal majesty.

What an asshole.

I slammed the door but he pushed it back, I could see his biceps flexing under the Armani. It made me more wet to think that his body would be just as glorious as I had left it.

"I'll call the police"

I told him, matter-of-factly, because I sure as hell would.

"Chelsea,"

He made my heart stop. I absolutely loved the way my name rolled off his skilled tongue.

For god's sake, we were parenting a 22-year-old.

It felt illegal to be this turned on.

"Lucy will be home tomorrow"

"I know jackass, she's my daughter too" I stated too loudly and bit my tongue. I didn't mean to be that rude.

Leo was amused, "I thought... Er... Maybe you would..." He paused, his eyes resting on my cleavage and it made me hot all over.

"Why are you smeared in paint right there?"

I turned to grab my phone till he stepped inside and closed the door behind him.

"Can we have a normal conversation like adults?"

"A conversation?" I laughed him off, "I thought that was not in your dictionary"

His jaw tensed till my blank canvas caught his attention. There was just a blue blotch in the middle of the white paper.

"You know what? Okay, we'll talk. But tell me what you see in this first"

Leo stared at me like I had grown two heads.

"You said so yourself," He stuffed his hands in the pocket of his pants, "I'm not creative"

"Of course. How could I forget?" I grabbed my phone again and opened the dial pad.

"I just see a blue spot on a blank piece of paper. Nothing more, nothing less. If you expect me to say something poetic, that's your fault. After all, you know me, Chelsea. Better than anyone can and anyone ever will"

His words seemed to pull something in me.

Something that I had suppressed since the day I left the court.

That day, Leo didn't hesitate to kiss me before we left in different cars.

There was something seriously wrong with him.

He never gave me a reason.

I hated the way he kept me in the dark.

"Since Lucy's coming home, I was wondering if you'd like to be there. Well, you know, the last time she was with us... We were together"

I noticed that he was picking his words carefully.

But that didn't change the fact that he was a prick.

"She'll meet me here. I'm not coming back to your stupid place. Now, move!" I shoved him away from my canvas and tried replacing the blotched paper.

"Was I right?" He asked.

"About what?"

"The canvas"

"Are you blind? Can't you see that's the reason I'm changing it?"

Then, hallelujah, I saw him smile. Fuck, I heard him chuckle a little.

He had learned to smile more often as Lucy grew up. But hearing him laugh, let alone chuckle, happened once in a blue moon.

Lucy had made him laugh a couple of times. It was a sweet yet manly side of him. I had made him laugh thrice in the near-twenty years that we stayed married.

First, it was during the hottest, most miserable night of my life while Jim was still alive. He chuckled while we were having sex as we both were immensely drunk.

Second, the Halloween costume that Lucy picked out for me was stupid. I looked like a pirate and Lucy pointed out that my boobs stuck out, and I told her that the best pirates had boobs. He laughed at that. Maybe that was his best laugh yet.

Third, an incident when Lucy was in her teen years and I was dirty talking the shit out of Leo till she heard all of it and I literally fell into the pool wanting to die. Leo laughed and picked me up, stripping my clothes off of me and wrapping a towel around my body. He was so sweet then.

"Will you be there?"

He had stepped dangerously close to my back and I could feel his breath on my shoulder.

"No"

"Why?"

"Why? Because we are divorced! That's why! End of story! Now get out, it's your bedtime!" I turned to snap at him.

"You have become pretty... Hot tempered..."

"I hate you so much and I want you to leave my life. If you take one more step towards me or try meeting me ever again, Mr.Xander, I'll call the cops. I'm not joking"

Leo tilted his head, those pale green eyes looking absurdly beautiful as a curled end of his hair fell over his forehead.

"I wish you were married to someone"

Did he hate me that much?

"What...?"

"Yes. Someone capable enough to keep me away from you"

His hand reached up to hold the side of my face. I was about to slap him but his voice sounded deadly, "If that warm hand of yours touches me, I swear, I will throw you on that bed and do god knows what"

Oh fuck yes.

I mean no!

Fuck no.

Leo bent his head so that his lips were right next to mine but he wasn't touching me. The very feeling of his hand on my face left goosebumps down my back.

"You still smell good" He whispered.

His breath was hot like fire. It burned me— physically, mentally, and sexually.

"Guess I should have kept you"

Those little words altered everything in the moment.

"Guess?"

I pulled away from him. Steady again. Furious as fuck. Ready to grab the knife.

"I can't have this conversation anymore. I'm tired. So damn much. Get out of my house" I choke on the last words.

"Chelsea-"

"Don't you dare say that! Don't Chelsea me for every stupid request of yours! Get the fuck out!" I yelled at him while pointing at the door.

Leo tried to step towards me and this time I didn't hold back.

I slapped him.

Even though it felt nothing compared to the slap that he had left on my face years back, it was strong enough to make him freeze and look at me with those cold meaningless green eyes.

"Get. The. Fuck. Out. My time is more worthwhile with someone else than you"

Leo didn't say anything for a while but his eyes were piercing into mine. Killing me.

Maybe... He might slap me back. Or hurt me even more... It's not like he wasn't physically incapable of something far worse.

"With someone else? You're seeing someone?"

I didn't know how he ended up drawing that conclusion but I preferred playing along.

"Yeah and can you believe it? He's actually nice to me and we have conversations. Note the word down"

He made no comment, fixed his tie, and was about to step outside.

"But no one will fuck you like me" I heard him grumble. Leo kicked the bucket of rich Belgium paint on his way out. I was saving that for later.

It was red. It splashed everywhere.

And he left.

Just like that.

Even though I swore not to, I took my diamond ring from the dressing table and squeezed it in my fist. The tears poured down quickly and I sobbed myself to sleep.

Why did it have to end like this?

Lyrics: I Quit Drinking by LANY and Kelsea BalleriniLast Edited: 15/11/23

4: yearn

"And you're not hereAnd there's no one to blame but the drink in my wandering handsForget what I saidIt's not what I meantAnd I can't take it back, I can't unpack the baggage you left"

~-~-~

It was raining outside and Chelsea wasn't in my bed anymore.

But there was someone else.

Her tiny leg was sprawled over my stomach while she clutched the stuffed bunny in her arms. Lucy was right next to me, wide awake and staring into my soul with her green eyes.

"Daddy you're up!"

She immediately climbed over my naked torso. My six-year-old was getting heavy. I sighed.

"Where's your mother?" I asked, often it was Chelsea who poked me awake.

"She's making breakfast. Mommy asked me to wake you up. Let's go downstairs!"

She jumped off me again and waited impatiently by the door. I sat by the bed, recovering from my three-hour sleep but Lucy waited for no one. She grabbed my hand and pulled me off the bed.

Soon enough I found myself being dragged down the stairs towards the kitchen. Chelsea was there, cooking in only my shirt and a pair of shorts. I dragged a chair and sat at the kitchen island, watching the rain till Lucy pulled me out of my trance by climbing onto my lap.

"Why did you wake him up, Lucy?" Chelsea sighed, "You know your dad is tired from the flight"

"But... But I let him sleep... For so long... And he promised to play with me today. Right Daddy?" She pressed her hands against my chest, staring at me with those big eyes. How could someone say no?

"Right. But you shouldn't have lied that your mother called me"

"I'm sorry" She shrunk back down on my lap.

Chelsea chuckled at this, "Wanna help me make some sandwiches?"

"Yes!"

Lucy rushed towards her mother. She lifted our little girl onto the kitchen island and handed her the jar of butter. "Spread it evenly" Chelsea smiled and helped Lucy with the knife.

"Do you want some, Daddy?" My cupcake asked.

I walked over to them and stood behind Chelsea, resting my hand on either side of her.

"Say aah!"

I smiled and did as told. She got all her mannerisms from Chelsea.

Taking a bite out of Lucy's bread, I pressed against Chelsea's behind. She glanced at me, a devilish smile tugged her lips.

"I thought you were tired?"

"Think again" I rasped in her ear.

My erection was already begging to be set free and her ass wasn't helping. I spent a week and a half in Spain but couldn't take my girls as Lucy had school and Chelsea had a studio to run. The flight was early this time, too early... And I had to groggily enter the comfort of my home at 3 fucking am. My sleep was destroyed, especially since Chelsea and I had an hour-long senseless makeout session as soon as I reached back.

Now, half an hour past seven, I was dying to be inside her.

But I reminded myself that I had held back before.

For a whole two months.

Even though the morning after ended with both of us severely bruised and immobile.

Planting soft kisses on her neck wasn't my thing but I couldn't take it rough and spread her legs here, not while Lucy was right next to us, of course. She has already done a fair amount of cockblocking for a six-year-old.

"Can we play in the pool?" Lucy asked while licking the butter off the bread. Children had such strange habits.

"Mm, if your mom's wearing a bikini, we just might"

Chelsea chuckled at this.

"Daddy's clever" Lucy replied, smirking.

"Why's that?"

"He wants you to wear a bikini to see your boobies. He hasn't seen them for two weeks" She literally pointed at Chelsea's bosom. I laughed while resting my head against Chelsea's shoulder. She had turned as red as the wallpaper in my study.

"I told you not to say that word, Lucy!"

Lucy was giggling, "Daddy says it all the time"

"Leo! I've told you a million times-"

"She's not wrong" I replied and brushed my lips on her neck. I could already feel the goosebumps on her skin.

"Daddy always says that mommy's boobs are the best" Lucy jumped off the island and squealed while running over to the living room. I wrapped my arms around Chelsea's waist before she could chase our daughter.

"Let me go" She groaned.

"You don't want this?" I ground my erection against her ass.

"You shouldn't tell the b-word in front of her!"

"I can't decide on what the b-word is..."

I squeezed her butt, "Is it this?" Chelsea nearly jumped. "Or this?" My hands ran up her shirt, squeezing her bare breasts and pinching her nipples.

"Ah..." She gasped and clung to the white marble.

"Mommy-"

Before Lucy could emerge from the living room, Chelsea pulled away from my hands and stepped towards our cupcake.

"-Will you wear a bikini and play with me and Daddy?"

"Once the rain dies down, yes. But for now let's do your homework and watch your favorite movie, okay?"

She beamed at the mention of homework, Lucy loved doing her basic maths. Gary on the other hand, would have puked. He was the most irresponsible brat in the world. But I was glad that Danny wasn't like him.

"We have to draw an elephant for school tomorrow" Lucy bounced around while getting her bag from the couch, "Then there are three questions on subtraction" She held out her book for Chelsea to view.

"Where are you going, Daddy?" She immediately turned to me.

I had hoped to sneak away and squeeze in a few more hours of sleep, but my daughter was too adamant. "You can wake me up when you're done with homework and the movie" I replied.

"No" She groaned, "You can sleep here!" She pointed at the couch.

"Fine..." I sighed and laid down beside them.

Sometimes Chelsea's hand would run through my hair or caress my face. I was beginning to feel attached to how warm her body was, inside and out.

~~~

So much smoke.

It seeped through my every cell.

It felt so damn good.

I couldn't give up on the habit. Maybe it was just how Chelsea liked to put it, "When you feel fucked up, you smoke. Don't you?"

It was just a distraction.

A distraction from the fucking mess my life had become.

Lucy was with me and I was supposed to feel happy. But I felt terrible because she couldn't return to a home where both her parents were happily married.

My baby didn't deserve this.

All her life, she had been perfect for our sake and I was proud of it. That was the very reason I thought of talking things out with Chelsea. I wanted us to be perfect for her. But balancing both Lucy's and her mother's happiness was complicated.

My ex-wife was dating someone.

And I was concerned.

Fuck, I was so damn worried about her.

It wasn't jealousy— even though Jeffrey loved to claim that it was— I was genuinely distressed. I cared too much about her and I hoped that the new guy did the same. She deserved every bit of happiness just like our daughter.

I couldn't give it to her. At least someone else would.

Someone else should.

I badly wanted the new guy to love her. More than anything. And she should love him back, just as much as she loved Lucy. She should also realize that I'm shitty as fuck.

The latter, I guess she did but... A part of me was mad.

It was selfish but I hoped that no matter how mad she was, I wanted her to know that I was doing this for her. Only for her.

"Mr.Xander, hello?"

I looked up, Kelly was waving her hand in front of my face. She flashed me a brilliant smile, her pink hair falling over her shoulder.

"What?"

"Is there something bothering you? You know I can help"

The young girl sat on the white marble and crossed her legs. She was wearing shorts that were inappropriate for any workplace, and she flashed her thick beefy thighs gained from plastic surgeries and junk food.

"Mind your business"

I blew more smoke in the kitchen. Kelly's hormonal face was in front of me again, "It's my day off" She whined, "And you're back from work" She continued, my eyes flicked up to hers. "And we are alone" Her tone sounded more seductive, "Not even Lucy is here to bother us or–"

"Kelly," I stared her dead in the eyes, "Don't forget why you're here"

"Of course not" She chuckled, "I'm here to make the boss happy"

I ignored her.

Honestly, I hated her too damn much but Lara was sick. And this brat happened to be Lara's niece and her parents partially disowned her— I could see why— And Lara begged me to keep her occupied for a while.

In all the thirty-plus years that Lara had worked as my housekeeper, she had never made an excuse or begged anything from me. This had been her very first request, and the little seed that Chelsea planted in my heart had grown too much to ignore Lara's pleas.

Fucking Chelsea.

"Leonardo Xander... That's such a manly name, you know" The teenager tried touching my hair and I jolted back in my chair.

"What the fuck do you want?" I all but barked at her.

Kelly flinched, then mustered her courage again, "We both know what we want"

"I don't fuck children" I muttered and got off my chair before heading to my study.

She was practically a child. Hell, she looked just as old as Lucy. That was disgusting beyond words, and I was in no mood for sex— To think I have never wanted it after the divorce.

Until the night I went to Chelsea's apartment and nearly got arrested.

All the testosterone from three years ago had suddenly returned.

It was no lie that she was and would be the best woman in my bed. I had no desire to tarnish myself with some low-grade whore anymore. Even though I tried to be turned on by someone other than my horny ex-wife, it wasn't working.

Maybe it was because I was old?

Not a chance.

A day before the divorce, Chelsea was clearly sprawled in my arms ignoring the fact that we wouldn't be married by tomorrow. But at that point, I didn't think cared anymore and wanted to make the most of what I had to offer.

Since it was the only thing that I could offer her.

Lyrics: Falling by Harry StylesLast Edited -16/11/23

5: HIM

"And all I've seenSince eighteen hours agoIs green eyes and freckles and your smile"

~.~.~

It had been two weeks since I started working for Dad and it was the only thing that had been going well for me.

I'd leave in the mornings with him and we had lunch together. My colleagues and bosses were extremely nice to me. It was mainly because everyone was terrified of Dad, which was not surprising.

There were only a handful of people he had grown close to and he earned them during the freeze. The ones that truly stuck around made their way into his heart.

When I was done with my job in the evening, I'd probably drive over to Mom's studio or Annie's place and I would get home by the time Dad reached back.

He kept looking more and more tired with every passing day.

I even began worrying that his health was at stake but it was far worse than that. It was a heart wound.

When I asked him why he had gone to meet Mom, he simply answered that it would have been better if she had come along to pick me up from the airport. I didn't believe that but his mood had dropped so low that I prevented asking anything more.

Today, a Sunday, was my day off but I did accompany Dad in the morning. It would be nice to get a headstart for the week and I organized my schedule likewise. In a few hours, I was done and went up to his room to inform him that I was leaving. Gary said that he had a surprise for me and I was itching to know what it was about.

I entered after knocking and just like that, I froze.

He was there.

None other than the great, popular neurologist- Danny Wilson.

And he looked nothing like I remembered.

Silky wavy golden brown hair and the perfect stubble. Mild brown eyes were staring back at me, his lips parted just as stunned.

Or I looked terribly ugly for him to stare hard.

Either way, Danny was dumbstruck.

"Are you leaving, Lucy?" Dad asked.

"Huh... Oh, yeah... It's good to see you again, Danny" I smiled, trying to be polite.

"Y-Yeah..." He replied, returning a nervous smile.

Puberty hit him so late. So damn late.

His voice had turned thicker and I liked it a bit too much.

After making out years ago, I had rarely met Danny. Probably because he was always busy with work. The last time Dad talked about him, he was busy with a research paper for a medical magazine.

Yet, that was no excuse to keep avoiding me at all the parties. We made small talk here and there but as usual, our conversations were numbered.

"I was just going out to meet Gary" I turned to Dad.

"Did he call you too?" Danny asked, surprised.

"Yes, he just texted"

"Do you know what it's about?" Dad asked, getting worried. He always expected the worst when it came to Gary but that was just his fatherly instincts kicking in.

"I really don't know... But," Danny turned back to me, "Would you like to go together?"

I was startled by this offer.

"Uh... Okay"

"Text me, alright? I want to know what it's about" Dad told us. After pecking his cheek, I followed Danny outside.

This was so awkward.

Especially since the elevator was empty with just the two of us.

"So... Mr.Xander told me that you began working here. That's great news. How do you like it so far?" He glanced at me.

"It's pretty good" And I briefed him on my daily schedule.

Again, there was an unsettling silence between us.

"And you? How come you're in town?"

"Well, I just got back from Illinois yesterday evening. I had a conference to attend here. After Gary's call, I thought of staying a bit longer.

You know, I haven't been home much. Guess I missed it..." He was staring at me now, his eyes turning slightly dark.

Danny cleared his throat and looked away, "So, I'll be staying for a while"

I hummed.

And again we turned quiet.

It really sucked when two introverts ended up together.

***

We drove together in his blue convertible. The car was amazing but the ride was not. We both were mute, completely.

I didn't know why there was so much tension.

Was it because he grew somewhat— no, a lot— hot?

Danny was getting all sorts of glances as we stepped into the restaurant. Suits and golden purses were everywhere, of course, this place was rich.

The waiter led us to a far corner. Gary was there with the woman I had seen in the news- Tania Fernandez, a sports show host. "C'mere you!" Gary pulled his brother in a tight bear hug and kissed my cheeks. His British ways had become permanent.

"You must be Tania" Danny shook her hand, "In the flesh" She grinned back.

"Gary's talked so much about you" I smiled and took a seat next to Danny.

"Damn, I've wanted y'all to meet for such a long time!" Gary chuckled. Making small talk about my job, Danny's growing reputation, and the footballer's future games, we had a great lunch.

"Show them babe" Gary smirked at Tania.

A light blush crept into her cheeks and she held out her hand. It didn't make sense why I hadn't noticed the beautiful ring before.

"You're engaged!" Coming from Danny's mouth, it was more of a statement than a question.

"How much longer could I wait?"

Pulling Tania's hand, her fiance kissed it. They were so cute together. Wild and beautiful in the best way possible. I was ecstatic to think that Gary had completely abandoned his flings and settled for someone more permanent.

"You look so good together" I smiled at them, "Congratulations!"

We talked about the party that they were planning to throw next month. Gary said that the wedding would be much later. He had a league match in a few months and Tania was waiting for her promotion. Once things get settled, they will fix the date.

"Dad is going to have the shock of his life" I chuckled.

"God, he's going to roast the absolute crap out of me" Gary groaned.

***

Danny dropped me off at Mom's studio and went home. As expected we didn't exchange much and I just couldn't put my finger on the fact that we were basically strangers with history.

I didn't know about his history of relationships but I knew for a fact that I stole his first kiss.

At least that's what Gary told me.

Mom was over the moon to hear that Gary was finally settling down. She was glad to hear that Danny was back too.

"Miss Chelsea!"

Patty barged into Mom's office while squeezing the phone in her hands. She was mom's assistant, quite a hardworking thirty-something lady.

"Oh right, I'm sorry for barging in like this, but you have to hear this!"

"Catch your breath first, Patty" Mom squeezed her shoulders.

"Hah... Yes... Er, hi Lucy"

"Hi," I chuckled.

She panted for a while then cleared her throat, "Mr.Rafael will be there!"

Mom's jaw dropped and it did hit the floor.

"He did not..." She gasped.

"He did!" Patty squealed.

Even Mom squealed.

They looked absolutely like two teen girls discussing their crush.

"Who's Mr.Rafael?"

"The Afghani painter! He's coming to the exhibition in two weeks. I never imagined he'd agree but I had my fingers crossed! This is so big for us Lucy!" She hugged me.

"That's great Mom!" I hugged her back.

"Oh my god," She turned back to Patty, "This means we have to work extra hard. Sofiana has to be the best exhibition ever!"

"I'm on it" Patty grinned.

***

I was pretty jealous of Mom.

Her life was always so interesting. The people she met, the work she did, everything was cool about her.

When I was young, she taught me to draw but I felt like Dad's job was better suited for me, hence I went down that path. Even though I had no regrets, I wished for my life to be more colorful.

Now, I feared ending up depressed like Dad.

Annie's name flashed on my phone right then, "Hey-"

"Lucy! Beach party. Tomorrow evening. 5 pm sharp. The boys will be there including our little to-be-married football star. You're coming too. End of story. Love you!"

She hung up just like that.

I smiled like an idiot at the phone. This time, I'd be going.

The shell would have to crack into bits.

***

Gary had his legs on the coffee table while Dad grumbled curses after hanging up with Mathew.

"Chill boss, they'll get tired and leave soon" He shrugged without looking up from his phone.

"Listen up you idiot, do not, and I mean DO NOT drag your sneakers into my office in broad daylight. Paparazzi is the last thing I want to deal with" Dad growled.

It was admirable how Gary was able to sit there without being affected. Maybe it was because he was too used to being shaken up by my dad. "Fine... I just wanted to see you in person because I missed you" Gary smiled and I struggled to hold back my laughter.

"You'll be out of here in five minutes"

"Sure, sure" He raised his hands in surrender.

Dad turned to me, his brows still creased, "Now, why are you here Lucy? Are you going to the studio?"

"Uh... No... Annie invited me to this beach party and-"

"You're not going are you?" He asked while taking off his reading glasses.

"I want to go Dad..."

"There are going to be drugs, drinking, and boys. I don't want any of that affecting you. It's for your well-being"

I wish I was stronger. Just a little bit stronger so I could stand up to him.

"With all due respect Mr.Godfather, you can't restrict her. She's a grown-ass woman"

"I didn't ask your opinion" Dad shot Gary a death glare.

"Lucy, do you want to go?" He sighed.

I fidgeted with the edge of my blazer, "Kind of... Yeah..."

Dad averted his cold gaze onto me, oh god. How did Mom even put up with this for nineteen years?

"Lucy, you're old enough to make your decisions and you know that this is a bad one"

"I... But I've never been to a beach party before..." I gulped, "I swear I won't get high or drunk"

Dad ran a hand through his hair and let out a deeply exhausted sigh.

"Will Danny be there?"

"Yup," Gary replied for me.

"I'll ask him to keep an eye on you, and you'll text me every hour so that I know you're safe. Alright?"

"Yeah," I smiled. It was proving difficult to conceal my excitement.

"And no strange guys... Or girls. It's the twenty-first century, you can never be too careful" He shook his head, "Most importantly, you'll be back by nine"

"Ten!" Gary grinned and threw his arm around my shoulder, "See you later pops"

"Take your hands off of her" I heard Dad shout as Gary dragged me out of the room.

"Choose wise adventurer, running through the paparazzi in the rain or sneaking out of the fire exit in stealth mode?"

I chuckled at how childish he could be.

Lyrics: Everything has changed by Taylor Swift and Ed Sheeran

Last Edited - 19/11/23

6: Taste

"I miss the way that you looked in your sundress The way that you looked when you undressed The sound of your first steps across the room"

~-~-~

Annie's boyfriend, Charles, rented a private beach and the party would be held there. They managed to invite so many people, especially with the trademark that Gary Wilson would be attending it.

The music was great, and there were crowds of people around Annie's age. I looked like a seventeen-something kid in the middle of a crowd consisting of hunks and big-breasted gorgeous women. But Annie caught on to the fact that I'd be a lonely weasel. She pulled me with her to dance. I was giddy with happiness.

The sweaty bodies around me were pretty disgusting but I reminded myself that this was what parties were about- sweat, happiness, and fun. Coming here wasn't a bad decision at all. I danced to my heart's content with Annie. There was even a karaoke showdown and Arthur invited me for a duet. By the time I left there, my voice was like a toad's.

"Ah!" I squealed when Gary picked me up in his arms.

"What are you doing?! Put me down!" I squirmed but he was all laughs.

"Oh my god, Lucy! Brace yourself!" I heard Tania shout. She was half laughing, half coughing as she came out of the water.

Before I knew it, he tossed me into the sea. I shrieked for my life. Gary collapsed on the sand and rolled around with laughter. "That wasn't funny!" I yelled at him as I popped my head out of the water, drenched.

Struggling to drag myself out of the waves, an arm wrapped around my waist and I looked up.

"You alright?" Danny asked. His soft eyes were twinkling in the dark. To my surprise, he was wearing beach shorts, and his shirt was unbuttoned all the way revealing his sculpted chest.

I knew that Danny was fit but not to this extent.

"Yeah, no, I'm going to kill your brother"

He chuckled at this, "If you're able to drag him away from her, I'll give you a hand"

I turned to look at what he was hinting at. Gary was on top of Tania, kissing her like there was no tomorrow.

"He's drunk, isn't he?"

"You know him," Danny smiled, "Let's get you dried"

We walked over to the bar, the cold air was hurting my skin especially since I was in Annie's borrowed bikini top and shorts.

"Here," Danny took off his shirt and handed it to me. As kind as always.

"Thanks"

He nodded and ordered smoothies while I stayed draped in his shirt on the barstool.

"I have never seen you this happy at parties before, Lucy" He smiled as he handed me my drink.

"That's because I haven't attended these kind of parties"

"What, really?"

"You know how dad is" I sighed.

"Hmm... Guess I should have seen the twenty texts coming" He replied while checking his phone.

"Gosh!" I buried my face in my palm, "I'm so sorry that you have to babysit me... This is so embarrassing..."

"Lucy," He placed his palm on my back, "Mr.Xander's just protective of you. From my pov, that's quite adorable. It can be overbearing sometimes, but you're his entire world. His only world"

I didn't know why but this conversation was making me mad.

"You all say that. He loves me, he's being overprotective 'cause I'm his only kid, etcetera. But think about it Danny," I turned to him, "All my life I've been his hostage"

"Lucy-"

"I wouldn't be the only world he's got if he wasn't so difficult. Mom was his world too till he pushed her away for no reason" I grumbled.

"He might be going through some stuff too-"

"You know what?" I snapped and pushed his hand off my back. "You're just like him, treating me like some kid"

"Where are you going?" Danny grabbed my wrist as I got up.

"I- Excuse me, please, I'm not in the mood anymore"

"Don't be upset. I won't say anything more. Stay, for old times' sake? Hm?"

Was he insane?

Sure, we were close as kids but did he even remember that he kissed me?

"No... I'm sorry..."

I pulled away and went over to Annie. After kissing her cheeks and hugging Arthur, I headed for my car. My phone beeped with texts from Dad and Danny till I eventually switched it off. I couldn't take this anymore. Driving over to Mom's place was the only thing I could think of.

At least she wasn't like them. She has always let me do things on my own. Sure, she was protective but she never crossed the line.

"Whoa, someone's in the mood to swim" Mom chuckled as soon as she opened the door. That's when I realized that I still had Danny's shirt around me.

He didn't deserve it anyway.

"That bikini looks good on you" She grinned as I collapsed on the bed.

"I'm so tired Mom. Can I sleep here tonight?"

"Of course, sweetheart" She caressed my hair, "Have you had dinner yet?"

"Not yet"

"Does pasta sound good?"

"Yeah," I smiled at her.

"Great!" She clapped her hands. It had been a long time since I watched her cook. She used to carry out all kinds of experiments in the kitchen even though Dad always complained that she was wasting her time. Yet, he'd be the first one to gobble up everything she cooked.

When I narrated his so-called rules for the beach party, she gave me a sad smile, "You know... You should call him..."

I shook my head and resumed eating. "Or you could wait here till he deploys the search helicopters" She chuckled, even I laughed at that.

"But I do mean it, sweetheart... Today might be a bit... Tough... For him" Mom mumbled.

"What's wrong with today?"

"Do you remember Grandpa Jim? It's his death anniversary" She sighed.

Oh my god.

That explained why Dad was in a crappier mood than usual.

Even though I've never had the chance to consciously interact with Grandpa Jim, Mom had told me all about him.

The way he managed to change Dad by working, drinking, and boxing together. They had so much fun together. He was a father figure for both my parents even though he wasn't part of their lives for long.

Ever since Grandpa Jim died, Dad had abandoned drinking. If my memory was right, Dad drank once a year and that was during his death anniversary.

"He'll be okay though... Don't worry about it..." Mom assured me.

I unlocked my phone and saw the near-fifty missed calls from Dad and a couple from Danny. I tried calling Dad back but it wasn't going through now.

"I don't know... I've got a bad feeling about this"

"Yeah... I guess you should go home once you're done eating"

I nodded.

[~ Leonardo's POV ~]

It felt surreal to be doing this again.

Fucking deja vu.

The last time I came home this drunk, was probably the first time I met Jim.

Home.

It wasn't even my home anymore.

After the divorce, three years ago, battling this particular day had been tough. Always.

But it was tougher this time.

Lucy wasn't answering my damn calls or texts. Being worried sick would be an understatement. She had absolutely no experience with how terrible the world could be and that was mainly my fault.

"Urgh..." I groaned, clutching the apartment stairs for support.

Even Danny had no idea where she was and he kept asking me whether she had reached home safely. Kelly told me that she wasn't there.

How the hell could she ignore me like this?

Why would she?

It made no sense.

Another something that didn't make sense was Chelsea's lie.

Of course, I couldn't let the fact that she had a boyfriend slide. I had to make sure that guy was... Well, my opposite. That he loved her to pieces.

But Jeffrey's private investigators confirmed that she had never been seen with any guy. Sure, she was at dinner with a couple of men but that was it. Her life blankly revolved around the studio and her messy apartment.

Why the fuck would she lie to me?

Why the hell wasn't my daughter answering my calls?

And where was Jim when I needed him...?

I lost count of the number of times I had pressed the doorbell.

"Who is it?" Chelsea groaned and opened the door.

Fuck.

Why did she always look so damn gorgeous?

"L-Leo...?"

"I've told you so many fucking times," I slurred, "Don't open the damn door till you know who's knocking. And don't lie to me, Chelsea"

"Leo what-"

"Shhhhhh" I stretched the word longer than I liked while leaning against the doorframe. My body wasn't at my will anymore. "You're seeing nobody. No-body. Fuck, with you looking like that, I wonder if all the guys have gone blind"

"Leo-!"

She shrieked when I attacked her lips. Kissing her with all my drunken libido.

Three years.

I had to go three years without her taste.

My hand wrapped around her waist, pressing her small body against mine, letting the door fly open, we stumbled into the cramped room.

I knocked something down, I didn't know what but I didn't care.

I wanted Chelsea so badly, to the extent of being completely oblivious to our daughter's presence in the room.

"Holy shit! Timeout!" Lucy yelled.

The second I turned my attention to her, Chelsea pushed me.

I thumped against the wall and crumbled on the carpet, face down. The world turned blurry in my eyes. Chelsea's panic-stricken face was the last thing I saw before blacking out.

Lyrics: Like Strangers Do by AJ Mitchell

Last Edited - 21/11/23

7: RING

"Little do you knowHow I'm breakin' while you fall asleepLittle do you knowI'm still haunted by the memories"

~.~.~

While sitting by the edge of the bed, Mom panted, "How... How is he... So freaking... Heavy!"

My phone was beeping now and I answered it to find Kelly on the other end, "Mr.Xander isn't home yet"

I rolled my eyes, she was only bothered about Dad as usual. "I know. We'll be staying... Uh... Somewhere else. You can lock up for tonight..."

"Somewhere else... As in?"

"It really does not concern you, Kelly" I sighed.

"Fine. Whatever" She hung up.

I hated every bit of her stupid attitude. Every bit.

"That bitch still works there?" Mom had her eyebrows up.

"Sure does" I chuckled.

She sucked an annoyed breath, "I don't understand why he puts up with her"

"Same" I shrugged.

"Have you seen them talking? Like... Anything besides work... You know-"

"Aren't you jealous Mommy?" I smirked and she rolled her eyes.

"You can sleep on the couch. Help me pull it out of the balcony"

We dragged it into the room together and after changing into Mom's spare clothes, I laid down on the cushions.

"Where will you sleep?"

"I'll be fine on the reclining chair. Goodnight" She kissed my head just like when I was young.

"Mom"

"Hmm?"

"Dad loves you"

She gave a humorless chuckle, "I highly doubt that, sweetheart"

"I know he does. He wouldn't barge in here drunk and kiss you otherwise"

My mom stared at me for a while, then began caressing my hair.

"Lucy... You're growing up into a wonderful woman and I'm so proud of you, but please... Don't fall in love with the wrong person... That stuff+... It scars you for the rest of your life. Promise me that you won't do something stupid like myself"

"You know, I was born because of that stupid something"

She smiled, "You were the only good thing that happened to us"

I groaned and turned away. Why did they have to finally burden everything on me?

"You know what? You love Dad like crazy and he loves you back but there's something seriously wrong with you guys. Why can't you just admit it and move on and stay happy like every normal family?"

Mom took a deep breath, "You should go to sleep, Lucy" She kissed me one last time before walking away. Personally, I was glad that the back of the sofa was turned against them. I wouldn't have to wake up to any smooches.

[~ Chelsea's POV ~]

By the time I was done reviewing the last artwork, it was a few minutes into midnight. Lucy was fast asleep, and so was Leo. All of us huddled in one big room like this brought back memories. Painful, bloody memories.

I sat by the bed watching Leo.

Over the years, his hair had earned a handsome wavy nature. A tuft fell over his forehead, gray like his stubble. But the rest of his handsome features were intact. Maybe he had become more tanned than I remembered.

That was when I noticed that Leo was sweating profusely. It must be the stupid alcohol. Turning him on his back was harder than I imagined. Had he always been this heavy?

I pulled the coat off of him and hung it by the door. After turning him over again, I began unbuttoning his shirt.

Shit, what was I doing?

We were divorced.

I haven't seen nor heard from him in 3 years and he was probably fucking Kelly for all I could care. On second thought, that was absolutely disgusting.

My grimace grew deeper when I had completely unbuttoned his shirt, leaving his chest in plain view. The hair on his chest had grown gray as well, but he looked hotter since I was a sucker for body hair. Even though Leo always said that my fetishes were creepy, he was very pleased on the inside.

All the abs that he had earned were there in full glory and my hand itched to touch them. To touch all over his body, just feeling every nerve and every muscle. His frame was an artwork of its own.

But what caught my attention was the thin silver chain around his neck.

I had never seen it before.

It was new and extremely unusual.

Leo often complained that jewelry was an unnecessary chore for the body. He never liked piercings or dyed hair or tattoos of any sort. And I still couldn't believe that he was keeping Kelly.

Scoffing, I thought of taking a better look.

At the end of the chain, there was something circular...

A ring?

My eyes were stuck on the piece of pure silver.

It felt like I was drowning all over again.

Was my vision deceiving me?

It really was the silver ring.

Our silver ring. With my name carved on it.

Why was he still keeping this?

I glanced at Leo who abruptly turned his head in his sleep, he was getting comfortable on my pillow.

My next instinct was to pinch myself.

And it did hurt.

Fuck.

Why couldn't the ring be just a figment of my imagination?

But it wasn't. It was all too true.

The great Leonardo Xander was wearing a silver chain around his neck. And our wedding ring was hanging from it. The wedding ring that had my fucking name carved on it.

When I let go of the chain, the ring rolled down the crook of his neck.

Nothing made sense anymore.

***

My Alarm was going off in the corner of the room and I slowly blinked my eyes open. It was aching everywhere, probably because I was on a chair and had slept with my head on the bed.

But that was when I felt eyes on me.

I stared back at him.

Leo was a few inches away, wide awake and quiet. The asshole didn't even bother to button his shirt and I had to internally sigh at the way his muscles flexed as he propped himself on his elbow.

Those deadly green eyes weren't looking away.

In a quick movement, Leo leaned toward me and I jerked back. The chair crashed on the floor and I yelped in pain. If my ex-husband was trying to be affectionate, he could at least try helping me up.

The asshole just wanted a second kiss.

"Still clumsy" He shook his head.

"Mom?"

Lucy rubbed her eyes and looked up from the couch. She froze on seeing her father button his shirt up and I was on the damn floor.

"W-what... What's happening...?"

"She fell off the chair" Leo pointed out.

"You caused this" I muttered and pulled myself back together.

Lucy quietly glanced at the both of us, "I guess I'll leave you guys alone"

"Hold it right there, young lady" Leo got off the bed, "I told you to text me every hour last night. Do you know how worried I was?" He frowned at her and turned towards me, "And you-" He slid his hands under my arms and helped me stand up straight.

"-don't open the stupid door without asking who the hell is on the other side. You know what happened years back!"

I felt my insides squish on realizing that he cared.

But he had no freaking right to yell at me.

"Leave. Right now." I opened the door and glared at him.

"Chelsea-"

Lucy wrapped her hands around her Dad's arm, "I think you should go home. Brush your teeth, take a shower, and do all of that"

"But who's going to tell her that it's dangerous to open doors like that? Dammit, at least install a peephole"

"I'm not your stupid wife anymore" I bit back.

Leo gritted his teeth. With his eyes boring into mine, he opened his mouth to spit fire but Lucy slapped her palm on his mouth.

"Please, Dad! Go wait downstairs. I'll be there after changing"

Leo gave me a last glare before stepping outside and slamming the door behind him. Even Lucy seemed upset and quiet as she changed into her old clothes. "Don't forget to return Danny's shirt" I smiled and hugged her.

Just as she stepped outside, Leo was waiting in the corridor.

"Why are you wearing a guy's shirt?" He narrowed his eyes on her.

I scoffed, fathers.

"Uh... Fashion"

"Fashion?"

Lucy nodded, "It has flowers all over it"

"Hmm" Leo inspected it closer, "Let's go"

"Bye, Mom!"

I smiled as she went down the stairs. Leo gave me a final painful glare before following her.

What the fuck was his problem?

Lyrics: Little Do You Know by Alex & Sierra   Last Edited - 23/11/23

8: Date

"Out of all the things I know nowYou're the most that I missed outRemember all the laughs we had?If only we could relive that"

~.~.~

"Why'd you kiss mom?"

Lucy asked while fiddling with the stereo. She left her car at Chelsea's place saying she'd get it later. Her silence did seem eerily strange in the beginning. Now that I heard the question, my grip on the steering wheel tightened.

"People do stupid things when they're drunk. That's why I tell you, don't get drunk. And who gave you such... Revealing clothes? Are all your bikinis like this?"

She rolled her eyes, "Don't change the topic, Dad. These aren't mine, Annie gave them to me"

"I don't like her"

"You don't like any of my friends" She crossed her arms and sulked. It reminded me of all the times she had done that as a kid. Lucy would sulk over stupid things all the time, especially when I refused to take her to the amusement park during bad weather. She loved playing in the rain too much.

"What are you smiling at?" She glanced at me.

"Nothing" I sighed and focused on the road, "I don't dislike all your friends. There's just Annie, Arthur and Gary. Maybe Jay too"

"They are my only friends" She muttered.

"Danny's a fine young man"

"He's not my friend!" She snapped, "He's like this stupid babysitter"

"Even better. He has a sense of responsibility"

Lucy didn't say anything for a long time, "Why'd you come over to Mom's?"

"I don't know"

Lucy raised her brow at me, "You couldn't have randomly chosen your ex-wife's place to crash for the night"

Sometimes, I regretted the fact that Lucy inherited her mother's smart mouth.

"You came over last night saying Mom wasn't seeing anyone and that she lied to you and boom, you kissed her!"

"I remember last night quite well, young lady. You don't need to remind me like some podcast"

Lucy laughed at this, "Why can't you guys just admit that you love each other and get married again? Maybe this time, take her to Hawaii"

Chelsea had to feed my Cupcake with all her romantic nonsense. I would never marry her again, nor would I take her to Hawaii. She could be doing all that with someone else and I didn't need to waste her time.

"We won't have this conversation again. Do you understand?"

She sighed, "Why are you guys so stubborn..."

"Lucy."

"Fine. I'm quiet... Like always..." She mumbled before staring out of the window.

[~ Lucy's POV ~]

Dad had a call to attend so after parking his car in the garage, he stayed there talking to the foreign investor. I would have to do the same in a few years. It ran a chill down my spine.

I headed up the stairs feeling exhausted. On nearing the kitchen, I froze on seeing Danny sit by the counter, impatiently tapping the table.

"Lucy!"

He hurried over and pulled me into his arms. The hug was tight, extremely. And I couldn't stop blushing because he was well-dressed while I was in a bikini for god's sake.

"I was so worried... Please, don't disappear like that" Danny exhaled down my neck. His warm breath made me shiver. It was so tender, yet I wanted to stay away from him.

"Sorry, I was with Mom" I mumbled and pulled back. This was what I hated the most about us. He always made me feel like a lost child in a zoo, "But I think I can take care of myself pretty well..."

Danny rubbed the back of his neck, his eyes were straying yet coming back to mine. Why couldn't he face me properly?

"I was just looking out for you, Lucy. Mr.Xander asked me to do the same last night but I was sure that you wouldn't do anything reckless.

You're the most level-headed girl I know" He gave me a soft smile—The classic Danny smile that melted the hearts of everyone he knew.

"Hah... Yeah..." I looked away nervously. Right then, I remembered about his shirt and handed it back to him, "Sorry that I ran off with this"

"It's fine" He chuckled.

Danny's soft eyes stayed on me for a while. Till he looked away again, "I'd like to make it up to you," He whispered.

"Would you like to go out for lunch?"

This, however, was unexpected.

"Uh..."

I fidgeted nervously with my fingers.

This felt like nothing compared to all the lunch and dinner invitations from Arthur, Annie, or even Gary.

"I'm sorry... I- I've got work... And..." I trailed off.

His face suddenly lost all glow, "Oh, I understand. Maybe some other-"

"What about dinner? I mean... I could get off an hour early or something..."

I didn't know why I brought that up. Guess, I was too used to accepting dinner invitations from Annie and the others that I overlooked the fact that I'd be alone with Danny this time. His gaze suddenly turned intense but warm.

Danny smiled at me, "That sounds good"

"Okay," I nodded.

What the fuck did I just agree to?

An awkward silence settled between us again as he stared into my eyes. I stared back, without knowing what to say anymore.

"I- I should go change. And take a shower..."

Danny's eyes momentarily flicked down my body and he licked his lower lip. It felt like I was burning all over.

"Okay. I'll pick you up at seven"

I nodded

***

As the hours rolled by, I began feeling nervous. So damn nervous. Not even my entrance exam made me fret so much.

What if Danny rethinks the whole dinner idea?

I checked my phone, thankfully there weren't any texts yet.

Maybe he was halfway through changing his mind.

He would probably text me saying he has other plans. Maybe he wouldn't text me at all. Maybe he would forget it completely.

Gosh.

I shouldn't have agreed to this in the first place.

By the time it turned 6.45 pm, my hands were sweating and I felt so stupid. He had definitely forgotten about me. But a text lit up my screen right then.

Danny: Hey Lucy, I'm outside. You don't need to hurry with your work, I can wait.

Why does he always sound so incredibly polite and sweet?

I instantly reminded myself that Danny had kissed me without consent six years back. He hadn't even apologized for that. Hell, he could barely hold a proper conversation ever since that day.

Well, neither could I.

But tonight, I was having dinner with him.

Like a date.

My first freaking date.

Even though I hated the fact that he was taking away my firsts one by one, I was too nervous to care.

My clothes weren't even proper for the occasion. I was in my sweater and a pair of black jeans. Annie's bikini was far better than my entire wardrobe.

The major problem, however, would be my father. I wasn't going to tell him that I'd be having dinner with Danny. My dear Dad would probably ask Danny to babysit me in the restaurant as well. I wouldn't be able to stand that.

I could lie that I'd be with Annie.

He'd hate it more but at least I'd have some peace of mind.

I knocked on Dad's door and lied perfectly. It was a skill that I had mastered over the years under his scrutiny. Even though I was always left feeling guilty, I couldn't help it.

"Be home soon, okay?"

"Okay. I love you" I blew him a kiss.

He smiled at me, "I love you too, Cupcake"

I wish he'd admit those three easy words when it came to Mom.

As I hurried downstairs, I noticed that it was five minutes past seven. I saw Danny in the distance. He was wearing a button-down white shirt, suit pants, coat, and no tie. As always, he managed to look dashing. Warm brown eyes fell on me as I went down the stairs to greet him. Right then, somebody bumped against my arm.

"Damn, Lucy. Didn't see you there" Jay replied, picking up the file and papers that he had dropped. I helped him while trying to hide my blush. The stupid handsome doctor distracted me.

"When did you get back?" I asked, handing Jay the last piece of paper.

"A few hours ago. Can you believe it? Your father is such a darling. He loves ruining my quality time with Mathew" He sighed. I chuckled at his words.

"Hey there, Jay" Danny had walked up to us, smiling politely at the older man.

"Good heavens! What happened to your face?!" Jay gasped.

Danny immediately ran a hand over his cheek, "Is there something on my face? Is it plaster-?" He asked, wide-eyed.

"Dear boy, where's Danny?"

"W-what...?"

"Stop messing with him" I laughed.

"You've suddenly turned into a hot piece of ass"

Even though it was dark, I saw that Danny was flustered. He was pretty adorable.

"Well, we should be leaving now" He turned to me.

"Yeah... We're going out for dinner"

"Ah," Jay gave us a sly grin.

"And I've told Dad that I'll be with Annie..." I mumbled.

"Noted" Jay winked before running up the stairs.

"Are you sure that... Lying is safe?" Danny gulped, "I mean, Mr.Xander... He..."

"It's fine for now" I smiled at him even though I was a nervous wreck on the inside.

Danny nodded and we climbed into his car. During the drive, we made small talk about our day. Surprisingly, it felt very easy to talk to him about everyday things. He was always smiling at me, no matter what I rambled about. Sometimes he stared too much making me worry that I looked too ugly.

Even though we were fine like this— friends or whatever 'this' was— A part of me badly wanted to know why he had kissed me that day.

Why didn't we ever talk about it? Or why did we begin ignoring each other completely? Even though we were close as kids. Why did we have to drift apart slowly with time?

It hurt so much to think that he might not have enjoyed the kiss at all.

"You okay?" Danny placed his hand on my knee, glancing at me.

"Y-yeah... Spaced out a bit"

He hesitantly withdrew his hand.

"Hmm. A penny for your thoughts?"

"Gosh, you used to say that all the time when we were young" I blurted out. Danny laughed, his wonderful voice was so carefree that it was beginning to make me relaxed as well.

"You used to say gosh all the time"

I stared at him. So many memories pricked my heart.

***

The restaurant was more posh than I predicted but it didn't feel awkward since we were used to this luxury. Dad never used to settle for anything less than five-star restaurants while taking me and Mom out for dinner.

The waiter led me and Danny to our table which was in an isolated corner. I preferred it because we were right next to the windows that revealed a wonderful view of the city.

"It's so beautiful from here," I told him.

Danny smiled, "Yeah..." His warm eyes were fixed on me as they reluctantly turned toward the menu. We ordered Italian and the waiter arrived with our food in a couple of minutes.

"Tell me, what do you do at home all day?" I asked him since the silence between us was growing too loud.

"Oh, nothing much. Cleaning up, organizing everything, honestly just giving the place a makeover. I haven't had so much time for myself in a while and it feels good. Maybe, I'll stay till the engagement party"

"Ah, that's great"

The waiter brought us a bottle of wine and I took small sips from my glass.

"And you?" He leaned forward, resting his face in his hands as he propped his elbows on the table.

"You know... Just normal work stuff. It must be pretty obvious that in a few years, Dad is going to completely leave everything in my care. Frankly, it's a bit overwhelming"

Danny smiled, "You're going to be a wonderful CEO"

I chuckled and took another sip of my wine. "Mom's having an exhibition in two weeks. It's called Sofiana. You should come. Gary and the others will probably be there. There's some celebrity coming as well, Mr.Rafeal I think"

"I know him" Danny nodded, "I've operated on his son once, there was a mild cyst in his brain"

"Mom is fangirling over him"

"He is a big name in the art world, it's no surprise" Danny grinned.

I few sips of wine later, he cleared his throat, "And you?" Danny gave a dry nervous laugh, "Do you 'fangirl' over someone?"

"I mean, don't we all?" I tucked a few strands of hair behind my ear as my face was beginning to turn red, "I think Belford Blue is nice"

"Belford Blue?" He raised his eyebrows in surprise, "Didn't he voice act for your favorite cartoon character when you were young? What was it... Ah, Tobby the talking racecar?"

I turned as red as Tobby's car paint.

"Why do you remember that..."

Danny laughed and sipped his wine, "It was all you would talk about, Lucy. Do you remember how Mr.Xander started to despise cars after you got addicted to that show? It was hilarious to watch him remember all the character names that you asked him to memorize"

"God..." I gulped down my whole glass.

"You were an adorable little thing" He smiled and tipped the wine bottle into my glass.

"I was ridiculed all through elementary school for loving a racecar even though I was a girl. Terrible memories. I think only Arthur thought that I was cool, he's always been such a sweet whacko" I laughed, finally easing up to my insecurities bit my bit.

"Ah, Arthur. I keep forgetting that you went to elementary school together"

"Kindergarten, elementary, middle school, and all through high school. Damn, we were always in the same class as well 'cause I was put to school a little earlier"

Danny hummed.

"Everyone thought that we were a couple. In the end, we did go to prom together every year just because Dad would never send me with anyone else and Arthur was so fun all the time. Since he knew about

Dad's rules, he knew that I would be allowed to go to prom only if he ended up being my partner. So, he never really dated anyone at that time"

Danny hummed again, his focus was fixed on his second glass of wine.

"Sorry... If I'm boring you..."

He looked up and straightened himself immediately, "Of course not. I just got distracted with something else"

"A penny for your thoughts?"

He gave a dry laugh and took a distracted sip of his glass.

"Nah... It's... It's not important"

"Aw, come on"

Danny stared intently at me, then turned away to look at his plate, "I was just wondering why you and Arthur haven't ended up together yet. You have a lot of history"

"Ew..." I blurted out earning a chuckle from him.

"Arthur's like a brother to me... And... Gosh, it's gross to think I'd want to go to the next level with him. He already has multiple girls at uni"

"Ah" Danny nodded, his mood seemed much lighter now.

The wine in my system knocked more boldness into me, "You don't have anyone special in your life?"

Danny pursed his lips and stared at me. He took a long while to respond, "I don't have the time"

"Hmm"

"And it's far too complicated..." He whispered the last words quietly to himself but I decided not to question it.

Lyrics: When We Were Kids by Bangers Only, Zeegs, SauceOnly and Preston Pablo

Last Edited: 24/11/23

9: Alone

"Every night I almost call youJust to say it always will be youWherever you are"

~.~.~

Mom was extremely busy for the whole week and I barely spent any time with her. Even though I went to the studio a couple of times, everyone seemed drowned in work.

This time, the exhibition soared around Sofiana, the central woman in every painting. It mainly expressed the themes of feminism and freedom, something cliché but beautifully drawn.

Art had always been a strange curiosity for me and Dad, even though we couldn't draw half as well as Mom. We kept away from brushes and admired the paintings only from afar. The last time I saw Dad draw was when I forced him to make the outline of a cat for me in kindergarten. He was so bad that we ended up doing it together.

Those were the real sweet memories.

All week, Danny and I didn't meet as he had to run some errands in the nearby city. He left texts though, sweet thoughtful texts that made me wonder if men as sweet as him existed. From my father's pov, every guy was horrible and their only agenda would be to get into my pants. But usually it seemed like he was referring to his infamous youth.

Mom had a broader perspective as she believed that every guy who approaches, deserves a chance. If they mess up but try to make up for it, they deserve a second chance. But if they make the same mistakes again, no more chances.

My parents sure were strange.

***

When Annie called me in the evening, I never expected that it was an actual emergency. "Lucy!" She winced in pain, "I think I broke my leg"

"What? Where are you?" I got off my chair at Starbucks.

"I'm at home... Gary's on his way here"

"I'm coming"

"Hurry" She winced again.

In a matter of seconds, I climbed into my car and drove over to her place. Gary opened the door for me. "I need a doc to look at my leg" Annie clutched my arm while her other hand was holding onto Gary.

"Let's go to Danny. He'll know what to do"

"Yes! That's a great idea!"

I cringed, as it made no sense why they were talking like cartoon characters.

"But isn't he neuro... If your leg is that bad, you should go to Rashmond-"

"No!" They snapped in unison.

"We are going to Danny's place"

"Yeah!" Annie replied, suddenly forgetting to wince and whine.

I was beginning to doubt if they were bluffing.

We went in Gary's car as he was the only one who knew the way. I hadn't been to this part of town much but I liked the neighborhood.

It gave vintage vibes especially since the sky had gone all red and purple.

"Is that..." Annie trailed off, gaping at the two-storeyed white mansion in the distance.

"Yeah, that's the one" Gary grinned and pulled over on the driveway. The blue convertible was already parked in front of the house.

"Let's go!" Annie squealed and hurried out of the car.

"I thought your leg was broken..."

Gary and Annie glanced at each other, "I guess it was just a sprain. Come on now! We came this far, let's crash here!" Before I knew it, Gary was buzzing the doorbell like a madman.

The door flung open with a furious Danny in a t-shirt and sweatpants.

"I fucking told you not to-"

He froze on seeing me, then looked at Annie who immediately began wincing. I rolled my eyes.

"I fell down the stairs and I think I twisted my ankle"

Now it was her ankle.

"That's why we came here, bro"

Gary had his arm around Annie again as he helped her inside, ignoring the fact that he just pushed past Danny. He sighed, then turned to me. I was still unsure of barging into his place like them.

"You'll catch a cold if you stay out there, Lucy. Come inside" Danny held the door open for me.

"Yeah... I didn't mean to show up on short notice..."

Danny smiled, "I don't mind"

But he did seem to mind when it came to them. So, why not me?

That was what I hated about him— The princess treatment. It was the aftereffect of having to babysit me for years, and of being my father's right-hand man.

We walked down the hallway after closing the door behind us. The house was beautiful. There were indoor plants in every corner, and the paintings on his wall were vibrant. Even the kitchen had a lovely color scheme, it looked exactly how Mom would describe her dream home.

Gary easily got comfortable on the bean bag in front of the TV. His eyes were closed as he relaxed to the music playing from the stereo system. "This feels like heaven," Annie sighed while leaning back on the kitchen counter. Gary hummed, refusing to open his eyes.

"It's a really nice place," I told Danny and he smiled back, "Thanks"

"Where are the drinks?" Gary pounced off the bean bag and marched into the kitchen. He was opening shelf after shelf and Danny was busy closing all of them. "There's only wine here" He grumbled.

Gary's face fell, "Man... You're no fun. Anyway, wine it is" He sat by the counter defeated and Annie rubbed his back with a chuckle.

"Seriously though..." Danny took out the fresh bottle of white wine, "Don't you have practice matches or something?" He opened it with elegance.

"I did and I still do but the coach won't mind if I take a teeny time off. He's pretty chill"

Danny wasn't buying it, he filled their wine glasses nevertheless. He even handed me a glass, our fingers brushing as I took it from him.

"Thank you..." I whispered.

"No problem," He smiled.

It was amazing how he could shift from glaring at Gary to being a gentleman with me. Over the years, I expected him to change his ways but no, it seemed to only get worse.

"I'm gonna go check upstairs. Coming Ann?"

"That's why I'm here!" She giggled and followed Gary.

Danny took a seat next to me and sighed, "I should've known that they would try something like this"

"Huh?" I turned to look at him.

"I told Gary not to come here because, as you know, he causes a hurricane wherever he goes." I laughed at his words. "He even made Annie call me and I had told her that it wasn't a good time because I was halfway cleaning. Now, they've brought you along because they know that I won't be able to turn you down" He smiled again.

I shifted uncomfortably in my chair, I had to change the topic. "Did you clean the whole house by yourself? I mean, it must have been pretty dusty"

"It was... Very hard. But I managed. Sometimes I think that I should appoint a caretaker or something since I'm rarely home. I prefer Illinois more... But emotionally, I can't let go of this city" Danny went silent as he stared at the floor.

I could see memories twirling in his eyes. Bad memories.

My parents had always kept me in the dark as to why Danny had suddenly become so reserved. But I knew it was something related to his mother's death.

Gary didn't know much either as it happened when they were young and I hadn't started school at that time. Mom and Dad asked me to never bring it up in front of Danny.

I could only assume that he was heavily involved.

The only thing I remembered from that night was Danny crying his eyes out on our couch and Dad was trying to comfort him. Since I was too afraid to ask anything, I stayed behind Mom while overhearing the conversations.

"Breath, Danny, breathe" Dad had whispered in his ear.

Mom had put me to bed early that night, and the next day my parents warned me to never bring up any questions in front of Danny.

Was he really suffering that much?

"I'm sorry, what?" I blinked at him.

"I asked if Mr.Xander minds that you're here," He chuckled.

"Well, he doesn't know..." I squeezed the wine glass in my hands, "And it's a Sunday. He has meetings all evening, so it's fine"

"Hmm... You don't want to look around?"

"No I... I'll do it another time" I flushed, actually nervous that I was in a guy's house and drinking wine. Even though I tried reminding myself that it was just Danny, it didn't ease me at all.

"Okay"

There was a sudden beep from the microwave and he got up to turn it off. "I was warming up dinner. Want some?" He asked and placed a plate of scrambled eggs in front of me.

"But it's your dinner"

"Give it a taste" He smiled.

With a lot of guilt and hesitance, I dug in and was thrown onto cloud nine.

"This is so good. Which restaurant is it from?"

"You're talking to the chef himself" Danny chuckled.

I flushed bright red, "Oh... I thought... Since you were busy... I- I didn't think that you cooked. I think I'm always assuming that rich men don't cook because Dad can barely flip a pancake"

He laughed at this and leaned over the marble, his face was closer to mine like this.

I took another spoonful of the eggs and hummed in pleasure.

Danny was gazing at me, his warm eyes never leaving my face. There was even a smile on his lips, one of pride and relief.

"Really, it's too good" I mumbled again. He grinned even more, leaning closer toward my face. His warm brown eyes were twinkling by now.

"Don't we get dinner?"

Gary came around, sniffing his way into the kitchen. Even Annie followed him and crashed on the stool next to me.

"I guess, I'll make some for everyone" Danny sighed.

[~ Leonardo's POV ~]

It was a very warm afternoon and judging from the clouds and humidity out my window, I could tell that it was going to rain.

Chelsea had her exhibition tonight.

Sofiana or whatever it was called.

Everybody was going.

But I heard it from Mathew.

Not even my own daughter told me about it.

"What do you mean, I didn't tell you?" I could feel her frown over the phone, "Why would you be there Dad?"

"Because you're there. Why can't I spend time with you?"

"Yeah, I'm not buying it" She replied, "You just want to kiss Mom again"

"Lucy!" I heard Chelsea hiss on the other side.

Only if she knew that I wanted to do much more than just kiss her mother

"Where are you now?"

"With mom. We're doing some finishing touches" She sighed, "If you really love art that much, I guess you could show up here... It's next to Mom's studio. There are posters all over the place, you'll find your way. I have to hang up now. Love you, Dad"

The door of my study flung open, revealing a cyan-haired Kelly. She was chewing gum and had her phone in her hand, "Aunt wants to talk to you-"

"Get out and learn to knock" I barked at her.

"But-"

"Get the hell out!" I yelled, the brat always made my patience snap.

She flinched and went out the door, grumbling something. She closed it with a bang, then knocked before barging inside again.

"No. Get out again and keep knocking till I ask you to come in"

"You can't be serious" She muttered.

"Get the fuck out and spit that damn thing out your mouth while talking to me. If you try anything funny one more time, pack your bags and leave dammit!"

She looked genuinely terrified this time. "C-Can I come in now, Mr.Xander?" She gulped.

"Come in"

She handed me her phone, "Lara?"

"Mr.Xander, good afternoon, I-"

"Hear me out" I muttered, "Your so-called niece is a pain in the ass. If she's going to be a bitch one more time, she's out of here"

Kelly snorted.

"I am terribly sorry about her sir... I know she's... Difficult to deal with... But it's the fault of her parenting and-"

"Save the sob story" I pressed my brows in frustration.

"Yes sir, well, I only ask you to keep her for one week. We're moving to Toronto next Sunday. Just till then, please put up with her. I'm so grateful to you sir, it's really-"

"Fine, Lara. Stop talking"

I handed the phone back to Kelly.

"You're finally getting rid of me like you wanted, huh?" She smiled after hanging up.

"Out" I pointed at the door.

She pouted. "Fine, I'll go. Will you be having dinner here though? Gotta tell Alvarez"

I thought again.

Would I want to show up at the exhibition?

Or stay in the comfort of my home?

Maybe the latter.

"Here"

"Noted" She grinned before bouncing out.

I sighed, Lara was partially right. Kelly's attitude and ways were all caused by her drunkard father and mother who left home.

At the end of the day, she was still a kid. Just like Lucy.

And maybe, just maybe, the ounce of patience that I reserved for her might be because I was used to parenting.

I had raised a little devil into a beautiful woman, but I couldn't have done it alone.

Chelsea was always there beside me.

Lyrics: Wherever You Are by 5 Seconds of SummerLast Edited: 29/11/23

10: Decisions

"We're only gettin' older, babyAnd I've been thinkin' about it latelyDoes it ever drive you crazyJust how fast the night changes?"

~-~-~

Dressed in my blue suit, I headed downstairs. Kelly's face fell as soon as she saw me, "I thought you were having dinner here?"

"I am" I pulled out the chair, "I have to take a file from my office after this"

"Ah!" She grinned.

I scrolled through my phone while eating till she cleared her throat for the umpteenth time. "What?" I looked up finally.

"Ta-da!"

She took off her apron, revealing the red lingerie that she was wearing underneath. I wouldn't lie, Kelly had a great plump body. Large breasts, ass, and thighs. Even though she was coated with fat everywhere. The five packets of chips that she ate per day were the root cause of it.

I stared back at my phone because it was getting distracting as Chelsea had worn similar clothes when I first met her in the club. The flirty smile, drinks, scent, and most importantly, the blood stain she left on my sheets.

I remembered everything.

Especially our life during the freeze.

She stuck around for so long. Loving me, Lucy, and our newfound truce that only included mind-blowing fucking. She stuck around even though I had barely anything to offer her.

"Come on Mr.Xander, we both know what we want"

I felt Kelly's hands on my shoulder and they moved down pressing themselves into my chest.

"Fuck, for someone as old as yourself, you're too hot. I can only imagine how big-"

I grabbed her hand, twisted it, and spun her around so that her butt was towards me. Kelly kept groaning in pain.

It wasn't a bad deal actually.

Fucking someone would probably end my sexual frustrations. Moreover, I'd be able to punish this brat to my heart's content.

But...

My years of chastity couldn't be wasted on a whore like her.

She'd be broken and bruised beyond repair. Literally.

Only Chelsea had ever taken me so wholly, surrendering every inch of herself, completely leaving her in my care.

That was what I wanted.

Not someone as young as my rainbow cupcake.

"It hurts... Stop, please...!"

I let the girl go as she turned around and rubbed her wrists, "You're into BDSM like I predicted" She muttered. Chelsea was the very person who taught me what that term meant. She knew a lot of fancy things when it came to sex.

"I'm leaving" I rose from the chair and buttoned up my coat.

"What's your deal?"

Kelly grabbed my hand with a frown and raised it to her breasts. I wasn't squeezing her plastic shit.

"I bet I know your kink" She smirked and let my hand fall as she pressed herself toward my chest.

"You're so bossy, aren't you, daddy? Do you want to spank me?"

I stared at her for a while.

Rage was something I knew but not to this extent.

Every syllable that rolled off her vicious tongue disgusted me beyond words.

But it was all becoming obvious now, her breath smelled like scotch. My scotch.

Fucking teenagers.

I pushed the girl away from me, she stumbled back and held onto the counter for support. I grabbed the glass of water that she had poured for me and threw it on the floor. Kelly flinched when the glass shattered into a million pieces, she looked away from the impact.

I grabbed her chin roughly, my fingers were digging into her skin and my eyes weren't forgiving anymore.

I could fucking kill this girl.

I wanted to fucking kill her.

Kelly seemed to realize it too because there was extreme fear in her eyes. She was trembling all over and her face turned as pale as a sheet of paper.

"Next time, my hands will be around your neck. I'll be strangling you while nobody— no fucking person— saves you from myself" My voice sounded deadlier than it did in my head.

"Clean this fucking mess, take your things, and leave. Never do I want to see your fucked up face or hear your damn name again"

I pushed her with more force and she fell back on the chair.

Just like that, I headed out to the garage.

***

The posters and signs were all put up as Lucy had told me and I soon came into view of the wide red carpet that led to the grand doors of the exhibition hall. Men and women with cameras were cluttered on both sides of the carpet. White vibrant flashes were everywhere as I got out of my car and handed the keys to a valet.

I was confused as to who was soaking up all attention but then I saw Gary, giving all sorts of poses along with his fiancee. When I walked over to them, the pesky flashes turned towards me.

"Oh my god!" Gary gasped.

"Move out of the way" I growled at him, then glared at the cameraman who nearly blinded me.

He chuckled, "You seem to be in a crappy mood but that's alright. You're here and I'm so happy Mr.Xander!"

The boy hugged me.

This might be the only reason why I allowed Gary to stick close to my daughter. He was affectionate and loyal, especially towards those he considered as family. I knew that Gary would go to all lengths to protect the people he cared for. Just like his brother.

"Mr.Xander! You've been very quiet after the divorce! Are you back to mend relations again?"

"Is it true that it's the stripper that you left behind and now it's the artist that you're back for?"

"Do you still love your ex-wife?"

Reporters. I wanted to snap their necks, especially the one who had dared to call Chelsea a stripper.

"Have a great evening!" Gary waved at them before leading me inside. His hand had snaked around Tania. Now that I saw her in person, he had a wild taste.

"You know how annoying they can be" He shook his head.

"Dad!" Lucy appeared from the hallway.

My baby was wearing a beautiful blue dress that fell to her knees. The diamonds that I bought her were around her neck as well. She was so beautiful.

Just like her mother.

"You're here?" She asked with wide eyes.

I pulled her into a big hug, "I missed you. I wanted to see what my daughter was up to. Are you alright?" I cupped her pretty face.

"I'm fine Dad" She chuckled, "I'm so happy that you're here. Mom's gonna freak out!"

I hugged her again. The conversation with Kelly was absolutely draining and holding Lucy comforted me in the best way possible.

"You're my whole world, Cupcake, you know that right?"

"I know" She laughed while inspecting my face, "But why are you acting so weird? Is something wrong?" Lucy clung to my arm.

"I'm fine. Let's go inside" I smiled.

***

I watched the multiple paintings that adorned the exhibition hall. They all had gold frames and glass cases. It must have been quite the investment to set everything up.

The room was crowded with viewers, buyers, and even musicians who played in the corner. From the corner of my eye, I even happened to notice doors that led to a dark room that seemed to have blue disco lights flashing from the inside.

"What's in there?" I asked Lucy.

"Oh, music, food, and drinks. Mom wanted a separate room so that no one spoils the paintings"

"Hmm, and where is that walking paintbrush?"

Lucy cocked a brow at me.

"What? Where's your mom? It's a basic question"

"Of course it is" She nodded. Now, that was my genes triggering her sarcasm.

"There she is"

I looked ahead as Chelsea stepped outside the blue room with a man. A much older man with wrinkled skin and pitch-white hair. They were laughing over something and I saw Danny beside them as well.

Chelsea froze on seeing me.

She wasn't the walking paintbrush tonight.

Instead, she wore a long black body suit that hugged her curves a bit too tightly. Her cleavage could be spotted from a mile away and the long cut that went up her thighs was enough to prove how daring she was.

Fucking gorgeous.

The older guy turned to me as well, his long white hair fell to his shoulders. I maintained a stoic face till Lucy nudged me, "That's Mr.Rafeal! The main guest"

"I didn't know your mother switched tastes to Grandpa" I muttered and Lucy laughed into my arm. Chelsea turned to talk with the old man and disappeared into a far corner with her assistant.

Danny and Mr.Rafeal walked over to us, "I finally get to meet you, Mr.Xander" He held out his hand and I shook it, "Mr.Rafael" I nodded.

"He's a world-famous painter" Lucy whispered.

"Ah" I turned back to face him, "Never been a fan of art, honestly"

When he chuckled, the corners of his eyes crinkled just like any other seventy-year-old. "You're quite... Raw, as the media says, aren't you?"

"I prefer honesty"

He smiled, "Well, I better look around more. Talk to you more sometime, have a good evening" Mr.Rafael turned to Danny now, "It really was a wonderful surprise, Mr.Wilson"

"Yes. I hope to see you around" Danny smiled and shook his hand. "I've treated his son once," He told me once the man walked away.

I looked around, "Is this it?"

"What do you mean?" Lucy stared at me.

"This small room... Paintings... People... Is that all?"

"Uh... Yeah, it's an exhibition, not a board meeting" She scoffed.

"You'll be heading a board meeting soon, young lady" I tapped the tip of her nose.

She smiled at me, "You should look around and I'll go tell the others that you're here"

"The others?"

"Jay and Uncle Jeff. Also, don't make a scene, please, this is important for Mom"

"I have never made a scene before"

"Whatever Dad" She rolled her eyes and ran off.

The bland 2D images seemed to be my only company until Jeffrey came along and handed me a glass of lemonade, "It's a surprise that you're here"

"Needed to clear my mind off some things"

"Hmm. You alright?" He asked, patting my shoulder.

"Yes, much better now that I've fired that teen whore"

He laughed, "Might be the best decision yet"

"I always make the best decisions" I muttered.

"Not much there though" He pointed past me with his glass.

I turned around.

Chelsea was staring at a painting, lost in thought as she sipped the glass of wine.

"It was a necessary decision" I muttered and turned away.

"Really?" Jeffrey raised an eyebrow, "When did the great Leonardo Xander forget about nightclubs, models, and mindless sex?"

I shot him a glare.

"When you met her, that's when. You're still faithfully committed to each other. Making my investigators stalk poor Chelsea..." He shook his head, "I've never had to deal with a more confusing case"

"Shut up" I grumbled.

"You're in love, Leo. You just aren't hearing yourself. Imagine how happy Lucy would be if you and Chelsea got back together"

"I said, shut the fuck up"

My mood didn't need to be ruined even more by his wise-ass words.

"The truth always hurts" He squeezed my shoulder before walking off.

***

Walking around the room, watching the paintings one by one, and getting refills at the bar continued for long hours.

Till I nearly bumped into Chelsea at a curve.

"You scared me!" She snapped and turned away to face a painting.

It was signed by her in the corner and it looked brighter than the others.

"I don't like it"

"Excuse me?" She frowned with her pretty face.

"It's blinding me. Too bright, too colorful"

"Not my fault that you're always a dark wreck" She muttered and stepped towards the next painting.

"I'm giving realistic remarks" I stepped towards her.

"Nobody asked for your opinion, Mr.Xander"

"Surely, you know me better than to imagine that I'm going to stay quiet about blinding colors"

She glared at me, "You know what? Maybe I don't know you all that well. How can I when you don't even give a reason"

Even while she was mad at me, I found myself smiling for some reason. It wasn't what she said, but the multiple silly arguments that we had had in the past years. Her tantrums had always been amusing, and I certainly did miss it.

I missed her.

Lyrics: Night Changes by One Direction

Last Edited- 29/11/23

11: curse

"If we're said and done I know, I shouldn't say thatI still care, but I still careAnd even when you're movin' on I hope you know thatI'll be there"

~.~.~

"Don't you have anything other than this lemonade?"

The bartender stared at me before glancing at Jeffrey who was chuckling on the barstool beside mine.

"Uh... We got pink lemonade?"

"What?" I scowled at the boy.

"Pink-"

"What the fuck is that?"

Jeffrey leaned back on the counter, and laughed even more. He was beginning to get on my nerves.

"Well, it's-"

"You know what? You're fired." I grumbled and leaned back on the counter.

"Are you really that mad?" Jeffrey nudged me.

I grabbed the cigarette pack from my coat and took a drag. Filling my lungs with smoke and puffing it before my eyes could at least blind me from having to watch Chelsea dance with the grandpa.

Ballroom dancing.

In a semi-club atmosphere.

"I smell jealousy" Jay's drunk ass quoted as he emptied another glass of scotch. His husband squeezed his arm before he could drink one more, "You shouldn't" Mathew sighed.

"I love youuuuu-" He eventually pressed his lips to Mathew's.

I turned away. These middle-aged scoundrels could get a room.

Another drag, more smoke.

"He was flirting with Leana earlier" Jeff sighed while taking a long sip of his lemonade. After my vow to stay away from alcohol, Jeffrey had thought of keeping me company and I was grateful for him.

"But she thinks that the old man is 'sweet talking'. How the fuck is that different from flirting?"

I scoffed, "Now, he's shaking his constipated ass with Chelsea"

Jeffrey burst out laughing while smacking my back.

"Watch out Mr.Xander" Jay mumbled.

I blew out the smoke in my mouth and turned to him annoyed, "What-"

"Dad"

I coughed, spat the cigarette out, and crushed it under my shoe.

"Yes, Cupcake?"

Covering my mouth by making a fist wasn't as smart as I'd hoped because Lucy could see through me quite well. She had her arms crossed and her forehead creased.

My daughter hated it when I smoked.

When she was in middle school, she had thrown out all my cigarettes. Ever since then, I had been cautious about smoking when she was around, but I forgot about it tonight.

"Hand it over"

I stared at her palm before making the most resolute face I could, "I don't know what you're talking about"

She took a deep breath before searching my pockets like a cop, "Lucy, Cupcake, listen-"

"Ah ha!" My little girl fished it out of my coat.

The men and I watched her in awe as she opened the pack and dumped all the sticks into a wine glass. She filled it to the brim with lemonade, "Ice" She glared at the bartender who promptly dropped an ice cube into the glass.

"Enjoy" Lucy sneered before storming off.

Jeffrey took a peek at the floating cigarettes, even Danny did. He had been too dumbstruck to speak.

"Well, she's creative," Jeff remarked.

"Now you know she takes after her mother" I grumbled.

Grabbing a glass of pink lemonade, I watched as Chelsea and Rafael kept laughing and dancing together. She glanced at me.

Well, my eyes had never left her.

It was going to be a long night.

***

Almost an hour later, Jeffrey was nearly asleep on the bar counter. Mathew had taken Jay home since he was absurdly drunk. Danny stayed with me, sipping his wine once in a while, quiet as always.

Chelsea was nowhere to be seen. Neither was the albino.

They must be cuddled in bed.

Crinkled in bed.

I scoffed, shaking my head, and drank my tenth glass of lemonade.

"Danny"

"Yes sir?" He turned to me.

"Never get married. It's a curse"

He smiled, "I'll keep that in mind, Mr.Xander"

"Good"

Even though a few seconds of silence passed between us, I felt the need to justify myself.

"In the beginning, they're all gonna think that you're the most charming guy in the world till you're married and bored. Now, a crinkly albino is more interesting. All women are the same"

"I second that" Jeffrey grumbled and plopped his head back on the counter.

"Or maybe... They were just dancing..." Danny chuckled.

"Shut up"

In the distance, I saw Lucy attempting to pull Gary off a couch. That boy was drunk and even his fiancée was trying her best to take him home. Danny noticed this and promptly got up with a sigh. He went over and helped the girls. The definition of a gentleman.

"You know," Jeffrey sat back up and rubbed his sleepy eyes, "He treats her like a princess"

"Who?" I frowned.

"Danny, with Lucy"

"That's because she's my kid. He's respectful"

Jeffrey emptied his lemonade making slurping sounds with the straw, "If you say so. By the way, isn't Lucy seeing anyone?"

"I'll snap his neck"

"It's the 21st damn century. They don't listen to us" He grumbled. It wouldn't take a genius to realize that he was referring to Annie's boyfriend. A younger college professor like herself but he had a well-off family.

"She couldn't have done better than... Argh, that damn boy!" He put down his glass harshly and got up from the barstool, "She's staying over at his place for the night and I swear, I'm not going to sleep"

"Shoot him then"

Jeffrey gave me a weak smile, "Unfortunately, I'm a lawyer and I know the consequences too well. My only relief is that he treats her well but still..." He raked a hand through his hair.

"When did we get so old?"

My lips curved up a bit. We had definitely grown old but if we hadn't, I wouldn't be able to take pride in how much of an angel my daughter had turned into.

Gary was leaning onto Danny and Tania as they walked towards us. "I'm going to drive them home," Danny told me, "Goodnight Mr.Xander, Mr.Campbell" He smiled at us.

"Can I go with them?" Lucy asked me once the trio had walked outside, "But it's already late. You should go home and sleep"

"Even Tania is a bit drunk. I don't think Danny will be able to handle them by himself" She frowned, finally making me agree.

"But Danny is to leave you home right after that. Alright?"

"Okay," She grinned and kissed my cheek.

Just as she reached the door, Lucy smirked and rushed back towards me. My daughter hugged me tightly before whispering, "By the way... I think Mom's getting drunk at Nightfall because of you" She pressed another long kiss on my face before running off.

Jeffrey laughed and threw his arm around my shoulder, "She sure is brilliant"

I didn't reply.

What was Lucy trying to gain from this?

"She's being childish"

"Leo, as a guy whose parents are divorcees, I can assure you that Lucy is trying her best to make your family whole again"

"It's not going to work, Jeffrey" I snapped, "She doesn't know anything. She doesn't understand how complicated things are. She's very young and stupid in this respect, hell, she could be thinking that love is a fairytale even now"

He sighed, "Talking with you is a waste of time. I'm going to find Leana and head home. Goodnight" He patted my shoulder before walking away.

There were only a handful of people left in the semi-club and the workers were cleaning everything up. I walked over to the adjacent room and saw that the paintings had all been packed away safely. Chelsea must have ensured that before leaving.

Mom's getting drunk at Nightfall because of you.

Nightfall was a recently established club that was famous for its highly intoxicating drinks and fancy atmosphere. For her to be drinking there, I might have put her in a tight spot.

Or was she wet?

Sure, I had kissed a couple of women in the months following our divorce hoping to end the yearning inside me. But none of them were as good as Chelsea.

The way she dressed tonight had particularly stuck in my head. Whenever she wore black, those nights had always been the longest.

I missed her curved legs around mine.

The thrusting. The grinding. The moaning. Pumping my fluid deeper and deeper inside her tight dripping-

Damn her.

I couldn't even focus on driving now.

Chelsea had put up with my tyranny for nearly twenty years. In fact, all the legal procedures for our divorce had been completed exactly a month before our 20th anniversary.

I remembered Chelsea being cheerful over nearly completing that milestone.

Till I ruined it all.

But it was for her. Everything I did was for Chelsea and Lucy.

My girls deserved the best.

And I was not that.

Mr.Rafael wasn't too bad on second thought. He was charming, funny, successful and most importantly, had a heart. But he was extremely old. And crinkly.

But who else could I entrust Chelsea with?

Who would be willing enough to put up with her childishness, sex drive, and mood swings?

My sole option which I had been searching for the past 3 years was Trent.

But where the fuck was that asshole?

No matter where I searched, it was like he had completely disappeared from the planet.

Or he was rotting in a grave somewhere.

But he had truly loved her.

He had made Chelsea happy.

And he could make her happy for the rest of her life.

My phone which was connected to the car via Bluetooth began ringing. The caller ID revealed the cause of my frustrations.

Chelsea.

I wondered when she had unblocked my number.

"You sick, sick, sick piece of dick. Hey, that rhymes..." She slurred. I had always been fond of drunk Chelsea.

"Listen you— shut up I'm on the phone with my ex!" She yelled at someone in the background.

"Anyway, dear Mr.Xander! I wanna say, fuck you! And thank you!"

"Thank you?" I smiled. She was certainly drunk and a new sense of pride washed over me as I was the cause.

"Yesss, thank you cuz right now I'm in queue to fuck someone. Copper-haired guy ten o clock"

"Good luck."

"What the fuck? Is that the best you can do?! My three-year virgin plea dies tonight and I'm going to take that boy home. Screw you!"

"Now you're fucking with boys?"

Chelsea yelled in frustration, "I hate you! I hate you so much!" She was on the verge of crying, "You're the most terrible, selfish, dickhead that I've ever met! And I fucking hate you!" Her voice cracked and she began crying.

"I love you..."

She sobbed even more. Those three words filled me with guilt again.

It had always been this way.

"And I swear," She sniffed, regaining composure again, "If you think I'm fucking with boys you better come here and fuck me like a man. Asshole." She hung up.

Fuck her like a man?

I would fuck her like a god.

Lyrics: For You by Why Don't WeLast Edited- 29/11/23

12: Attract

"I miss you when it hurtsI'm sleeping in your shirtsBut seeing you would make it worse"

~.~.~

I hadn't been to a club in ages and especially not somewhere with too many neon lights. It was crowded and I somehow took a seat at the bar.

"Just cold water," I told the bartender who nodded.

Scanning the crowd, I finally caught sight of a tall copper-haired lanky fellow.

He looked like a college student. Barely any hair on his chest. Chelsea made a poor choice this time. They were grinding against each other. His hands were on her hips as she kept grinning and pecking his lips.

"You got a cigarette?" I turned to the bartender.

He nodded and took one out of his pocket. I popped it in my mouth as he brought the lighter. A deep sense of fulfillment engulfed me as the nicotine hit my nerves. The DJ switched to a new Spanish song and the crowd immediately turned hornier, dancing and yelling around as the upbeat music flooded their ears.

I watched Copper Hair. He moved his hands down, tightly gripping Chelsea's ass. She chuckled, pressing her head against his chest with her eyes closed. Jealousy was childish and I had never been jealous of any of the guys that Chelsea liked.

Instead, I was protective.

They were two completely different terms. It was the same way with Lucy— to extended degrees though. Because Lucy was completely and wholly mine.

But Chelsea was not.

I never had and never would own her.

Still, I had promised to keep her safe.

That I would.

The boy that she was flirting with didn't have that sense of responsibility. Hence, I was far above him. As long as she didn't find someone emotionally stable and mature, I would keep taking these pricks out of her life.

Chelsea opened her eyes then. The guy had been erotically running his hands up and down her ass like it was the first one that he had touched. I could tell that she was bored.

She looked around until I caught her attention.

Her drunk face was suddenly flustered and stunned. She immediately turned away. I waited.

Chelsea turned to face me again, her eyes were filled to the brim but she was frowning at me. In order to taunt her, I tipped my head back and took another long drag of the cigarette. My arms rested back on the counter as I pulled out the cigarette. We never looked away from each other.

She tensed up a bit.

But immediately spun around, grinding her ass against the boy. He froze, unable to move as my ex-wife grabbed both his hands and placed them over her breasts.

He stood like a statue.

A chuckle escaped me as I propped my knee up, crossing it over my other leg. Bringing the cig to my mouth again, I basked in my smoky victory. Chelsea was beyond frustrated.

She pushed the guy away, "Wait, hold on, I'm sorry!" But she was already marching towards me.

Sexy.

I wasn't startled when she stood before me with clenched fists. Her face was bright red from anger, embarrassment, and drunkenness.

"What are you doing here?" She bit, trying her best to sound sober.

"I wanted to see for myself. A college boy? Really now?"

She huffed, "Don't be too cocky"

"Sit down and I'll show you how perfectly cocky I can be. Compared to someone who doesn't have a cock at all"

She pursed her lips as I took another drag and blew the smoke on her face, mocking her was pure entertainment. The next instant, Chelsea snatched the cig from my mouth and smoked herself. She scrunched her face while pulling the stick out of her lips.

This had been her reaction when I made her smoke for the first time, I smiled.

She took another hasty breath and cupped my face in her palms before crushing our lips together.

The unfamiliar taste of tequila hit me.

I reached up, taking the cig out of her hands without breaking the kiss. Our desperate tongues fought against each other. Her saliva dripped down my mouth and she seemed eager to go further.

I crushed the cig on the counter before letting my hand curve around her waist. Chelsea settled on my lap and I held her there. She locked her arms around my neck, but they moved up to tangle her fingers in my hair. I pulled her as close as possible, my hands had wrapped around her to keep her steady on my lap.

Chelsea pulled back, gently resting her forehead against mine. We both were panting. The makeout session might have left us even more starved.

"I thought you wouldn't come" She whispered as a tear rolled down her cheek.

"I don't waste my chances to see you drunk, do I?" I whispered and wiped the tears off her face. Chelsea looked like a mess from all the sweating, crying, and drinking. But even though she was blotchy, she was begging to be fucked.

"Um... Mrs...?"

Copper Hair was standing right behind us and he gave me a puzzled look. Chelsea didn't turn. Instead, she exhaled and buried her face in my neck. My hand involuntarily went up to caress the bare skin on her back.

I gave the boy a bored look, "She's busy"

He rubbed the back of his neck, shook his head, and walked away with slumped shoulders. Maybe that would inspire him to be more of a man.

"I missed you. So fucking much" Chelsea whined.

I sighed and hugged her back, "I might have missed us too"

The house was empty without her, my room was empty, and my bed was empty. My life used to overflow with her presence but not anymore. It wasn't a lie, I missed the warmth of her body so much.

Holding Lucy was the only thing that could feel this good.

"And you still don't love me" She muttered.

"Still won't" I assured her and pulled back.

Chelsea scowled at me, her face burning as she brought her hands back to my face.

"I want to fucking rip you apart"

You have.

"It's been a while since I had a taste of this feisty side"

"Oh, I'm dying to shine more light on it" She scoffed and palmed the bulge in my pants.

"I might bite this off"

"It's all yours" I smiled.

Chelsea grumbled something and shot up from my lap, "You're terrible, Leo"

"Yeah?"

"You're a beast" She muttered and walked out.

"Says the other beast"

I heard her snort as she walked outside the club and towards my car.

***

The drive was long especially since Chelsea had too much to blabber about. Every sentence that spilled out of her lips had an insult directed at me. At one point she cried into her palms and had the audacity to wipe her nose on my coat.

I was itching to spank her but I kept quiet.

When I parked the car, she refused to get out. I was forced to walk over to her side, unbuckle her seatbelt, and literally drag her outside.

"You can't do this!" She yelled while fighting my arms that were wrapped around her.

"I sure as hell can. And this too" I tossed her over my shoulder and she shrieked. I was glad that most of the tenants had moved out but at least two or three of them peeked out of their windows.

On seeing me with Chelsea, they pulled down their shutters just as quickly.

The power was rich.

"Put me down!" She yelled, "Help! Somebody help!"

I smacked her ass and this time she really yelped in pain.

"Don't make me throw you down the stairs"

She was completely quiet and I peacefully reached her front door. Taking the key out of her purse, I pushed open the door and turned on the lights.

"You're putting on weight" I muttered while laying her on the bed.

As I cracked the joints on my shoulders, Chelsea sat up with her arms crossed. She stared at me with tears in her eyes, "You're going to take advantage of the fact that I'm drunk, aren't you?"

"Obviously. Turn around" I commanded and she did as told in a defeated manner.

Her black dress had multiple knots on the back and I began undoing them one by one. Chelsea broke down into sobs without hesitation.

"Why are you doing this? W-why are you raping me?"

"You don't seem to be struggling" I sighed and untied the first knot with a lot of difficulty.

"Just because I'm d-drunk you're going to fuck me and throw me away in the morning. Just like you did for twenty years"

"Right. Who even tied these so tightly?"

"Lucy" She mumbled.

"That explains it" I sighed, even though she wasn't here, my daughter had indirectly cockblocked me.

"Leo..." She whimpered, glancing at me over her shoulder, "Why do you hate me?"

I glanced at her blotched face, "I don't hate you. It's the opposite"

She gasped, "Y-you love me?"

"No, I am fond of you. But if you continue spewing dumb shit, I'll begin hating you"

"Y-you... You don't hate me...?" Her voice cracked.

"Of course, I don't. You gave birth to my kid, raised her, and grew your own business with talent. Why would I hate you? Don't be an idiot"

Chelsea cried again, loudly this time. I was done with the third knot.

"I love you so much...! So damn much! And I miss you! And Lucy! I miss how we all were together!"

I didn't reply.

"Leo, you know I love you right?" She quieted down.

I hummed, done with the fourth knot.

"Why did you file a divorce?" She whispered, "Why did you want to end all of that if you didn't hate me?"

I was too busy with the final knot, so I ignored her. For a while, we both stayed eerily quiet. When it came off, I made her turn to face me.

"Why do you have our ring hanging from your neck?"

I froze and took multiple seconds to contemplate her words.

"You saw that when you were too desperate to get me naked, huh?"

"I was not!" She snapped as I slipped my hand into her clothes and pulled it down to her waist.

"What's your excuse for not wearing a bra?"

My hands brushed against her neck, gently tossing back her hair. I grazed her collarbone with my fingers, her skin was burning.

"Leo, why did-"

"Chelsea" I warned, "Do you want to keep playing damn twenty questions or do you want to be fucked. Your choice"

"I want both"

"Not a chance" I spun her around, my hands roughly grazing down to hold her bouncy round breasts, "You don't even have a choice anymore"

"Ah!" She moaned when I squeezed her, "This is not what you're supposed to do!"

I grazed the tip of my tongue up her neck, "What am I supposed to do then, hm?"

She shivered, "Y-you got to give me a shower, s-sober me up, put m-me in y-your clothes, and take care of me. Not take advantage o-of me... Th-That's what good men do..."

"Really?" I sat by the edge of the bed and spun her around to face me.

"Y-yeah..." She flushed.

"Excuse me for being terrible, as you said" My hands moved into the dress that hugged her waist and completely pulled it down.

"You can start by kneeling" I smiled.

Lyrics: Lost Without You by Clara Mae and Fly By Midnight Last Edited - 30/11/23

13: Repel

"The good champagne and private planesBut they don't mean anything'Cause the truth is out, I realiseThat without you here, life is just a lie"

~.~.~

I had my hand tucked under my head while Chelsea was lying utterly still over my chest. She was exhausted, worn out, sleepy, I didn't know what. She was too tired to even move an inch and hence, I was still buried inside her while my other hand ran through her hair.

"Will you walk in the morning?"

"Won't you be happy if I can't?" She fired back.

"Well, you won't" I assured her.

Chelsea struggled to pull herself back up and moaned as she did. She was completely sitting down on my cock and I watched her.

"My headache is killing me..." She groaned and tried to get up but I held her firmly by the waist.

"We aren't done yet"

I sat up and pushed her back on the bed. She whimpered at the slightest movement.

Grinding slowly at first, I slid out and slid back in with ease, she had already adapted so well in a few hours. Every thrust made her moan and I had my face directly above her breasts, watching them bounce was extremely satisfying.

"Leo! Ah, fuck!" She moaned louder when I picked up my pace.

The chain around my neck was a nuisance as it kept dangling about. I brought it to my mouth and kept the ring between my teeth.

"Fuck, that's hot! Stop doing that! Ah!" She groaned, throwing her head back.

A lot more thrusts later, I came inside her again and rolled to the side. I was already missing the warmth of her core.

***

I felt something, or someone, wiggle next to me.

"What are you doing...?" I cracked my eyes open to find Chelsea trying to escape from under my arm.

"Why did you let me drink so much! let me go!" She didn't let us spoon anymore.

Chelsea sat up while covering her naked body with the sheets.

"Fuck!" She groaned, "Leo what the hell are we doing? How could you do this?! I was drunk for fucks sake! We are divorced. Divorced! What is wrong with you..." She scowled at me.

I leaned up and gently held her chin with my fingers to take a good look at her neck.

"What are you trying to do?" She frowned.

I pulled the sheets away and stared at her body, thighs, everywhere.

"Haven't you had enough scrutinizing me?" She asked, her words tired and pained.

"I'm making sure that I didn't bruise you much. It's just a couple of hickeys and you're alright. How's your headache?" I caressed her cheek and she had a hard time looking away from me. Chelsea looked conflicted.

"You should leave" She suddenly got up and wrapped herself in a robe.

Fiddling the drawers for something, she finally took out a tablet and swallowed it with some water.

"Can you put on a shirt for Christ's sake!" She yelled. I never thought my physique would still be a turn-on for her.

That's when I glanced at my watch, it was half past six. "I have a meeting in two hours and I need to be home before Lucy wakes up" I sighed. The chain around my neck dangled as I pulled on my boxers and pants.

Chelsea narrowed her eyes at me, "Are you sure that you're going home for Lucy and maybe, who knows, some pink-haired bitch?"

I scoffed at her words while grabbing my shirt from the floor, "The so-called pink-haired bitch has been fired. Instead, it was the jealous ex-wife who's been fucked" My eyes rested on her exposed cleavage. The specks of hickeys were in plain sight, "And thoroughly at that"

She hugged herself tighter.

"Besides," I pulled on my shirt, "The last thing I want is to screw a whore after being alone for three years"

Chelsea looked stunned, "What...?"

I stepped towards the mirror in an attempt to fix my hair. Chelsea silently came over and began buttoning my shirt. It brought back too many memories.

"I don't think I've had sex in three years either" She quietly admitted.

Her hand left my collar unbuttoned as she pulled out the silver chain. Chelsea stared at the ring for a while, "And you've kept this... Why?"

"Brings good luck. Always has" I muttered and stuffed it back into my shirt.

Even though I had no intention of staying any longer, I found myself frozen even after I had fetched my coat.

"You know what?" I frowned and stepped towards her. As annoyed as I was, my hand caressed her face till my thumb made its way down to her lips.

"We need to get you married fast or I might just come over every night"

I forced my lips on hers but she wrapped her arms around me, pulling me closer, deepening the kiss till I pulled away.

"Dammit Chelsea" I grumbled before hurrying home.

***

Lucy must have been alone all night.

After parking my car in the garage, I raced up the stairs to find all the doors and windows locked. When I reached the glass doors of the living room, I saw Danny sleeping on the couch in the same clothes from last night.

What the hell?

I banged on the glass making him jolt awake. He hurried over and opened the door for me.

"What are you doing here? Where's Lucy?" I looked around.

"I think she's still sleeping upstairs Mr.Xander" Danny sounded nervous, "Lucy waited all night and tried calling you but you didn't pick up. Even the housekeeper wasn't here so I didn't want to leave her alone just like that. But while waiting, I guess I fell asleep... I stayed on the couch the whole time, I swear" He gulped.

I gave him a good stare, "And the blanket?" I muttered, gesturing to the cloth he was covered in.

"Oh... Uh... Lucy might have put it over me while I fell asleep... I honestly don't know"

I walked over to the kitchen and drank a glass of water.

He silently watched me, "Uh..."

"What?"

"Are you alright sir?" He whispered, "You look a bit... Tired?" Danny scratched his neck as though he was hinting at something.

I glanced at the curve of my neck, a dark red hickey peeked outside. Right then, Lucy decided to hurry down the stairs in her PJs, "Dad!" She stretched the 'a' too much.

I muttered curses under my breath and straightened my shirt so that she wouldn't see it. If Lucy realized that I was fooling around with her mom all night, she wouldn't let me live it down.

She was startled to see Danny, "Oh... I-I forgot that you were here... I'm so sorry. Did you sleep okay?"

"Yeah," He smiled, "Thanks for the... Blanket"

Lucy blushed a bit, "Ah... Er, don't mention it"

I turned to the boy, "You can head home now and whatever happened stays between us, alright?"

He nodded and said his byes before leaving.

"What happened though?" Lucy asked curiously.

"How could you let him in here while you were alone?" I growled back and she fell silent, "And that too you let him sleep here! Just because Danny isn't like other men, it doesn't mean that you should let your guard down"

"But where were you dad?" She crossed her arms and huffed, "Kelly's gone, that's great! But I thought that you'd be home by the time he dropped me off"

"I was busy"

"You've worn your coat inside out, I'm sure Mom would have loved the new style"

Even I hadn't noticed that. Fucking Chelsea.

"You went to Nightfall, didn't you?" A sneaky smile played on my daughter's lips.

"I didn't. Go get dressed, young lady, you have work"

"Right... Keep changing the topic" Lucy skipped back toward the staircase, "I'll make you marry Mom again! Properly this time!" She yelled before shutting her door.

***

It was around one in the afternoon and most of my employees were out to have lunch. I sat by my laptop while calmly sipping coffee. Lucy often popped up around this time to have lunch.

But a phone call interrupted me, Jeffrey rarely called in the afternoons.

"Have you seen the news?!" He yelled into my ear.

"My damn ears"

"Your damn ears? Your damn reputation is at stake here! Even Chelsea's! Just google up your name!"

Sighing, I did and choked on the coffee just as Lucy barged into my room.

"Dad! Did you see this?! You kissed, Mom? Again!"

My Cupcake yelled. At the top her voice. Nearly my whole company must have heard her.

The screen of my laptop lit up with the photograph of Chelsea on my lap. She was cupping my face, our lips pressed together in hunger, while the cigarette smoke made the picture quite aesthetic.

"Damn, you guys look hot" Lucy mumbled and I noticed that she was standing directly behind me now. Jeffrey was cackling into the phone.

Even Mathew came rushing towards my room and knocked on the door panting, "Sir, there seems to be a-"

"Do you need to ask me, dammit? Take it down for fuck's sake" I yelled and he shrunk like a wet kitten, "R-right a-away sir"

Jay appeared right behind him and flung an arm around Mathews's shoulder while glaring at me, "Don't you yell at him. He's all mine. After all, you have Chelsea now"

"Out" I spat at them.

"Mr.Xan-"

"Get the hell out!"

Jay closed the door after pulling Mathew with him.

"Jeffrey, are you still there?" I barked into the phone.

"Yep, hearing it all" He replied.

"Sue them. Sue them all. We made it clear to not use the term stripper. She's not a damn stripper"

"Is that what's got you so mad?" He asked in an amused tone.

"Just do as I tell you" I snapped.

He sighed, "I might as well get new marriage papers while I'm at it. Gotta plan a wedding you see-" I hung up.

Lucy sighed, "Why can't they at least say, artist... She's worked so hard and the stupid paparazzi got to use her past to get more views! I hate them so much"

"I'm going to end their careers"

I leaned back in my chair as Lucy gently squeezed my shoulders. When she was younger, she had the habit of giving me a massage whenever I got home late after work. She really was an angel.

"Dad"

I hummed.

"Why don't you just confess?"

"Because I don't love her Lucy. Stop asking me already" I groaned.

"Look, you love hooking up with mom. You prefer being around mom all the time. I've seen how cute you guys are, I've literally seen everything..."

The most terrific cockblocker of our lives.

"Clearly, you and Mom have so much history, shared trauma, and of course, chemistry. It's so obvious to everyone around you. Why won't you just admit it?"

"There are many things besides what you think you know" I replied before taking her hand in mine.

I kissed it, "We both have made too many mistakes. Some things can never be forgotten, or forgiven... But we put up with everything just to raise you. We have done that quite well, Cupcake. We don't need each other, we only need you"

Lucy silently looked away. Sometimes, I could never tell what she was thinking.

"Let's go out to eat, hmm?"

She nodded.

Lyrics: History by One Direction

Last Edited - 01/12/23

14: Stranger

"It's always like this It starts out so innocent Oh God, I hate what you did But I still catch myself"

~.~.~

It had been a couple of days since Mom and Dad hooked up, and I even saw hickeys on them no matter how hard they tried to hide it. These big babies practically had sex. Gross. But they still did it.

Even though they were divorced.

Only if I had half as much boldness as either of them...

Last night when Danny insisted on waiting outside by the loungers for Dad I had mustered enough courage to invite him inside. But the moment was ruined when we found a sticky note left by Kelly stating "Fuck you" in big ugly handwriting.

I was so glad that she was gone.

At least I wouldn't have to see any more thirsty glances sent toward Dad.

But I was used to it as nearly all middle-aged women (even girls my age) were drooling over Dad. He was hot beyond comparison. To be honest, I had never seen someone as handsome as my father.

And maybe that was the reason everyone complimented me on how flawless I looked even though I personally considered it a curse. Ever since I came to Xander Corp, someone or the other left flowers on my desk every day.

I hated the special treatment.

Maybe it was because I would end up being the CEO eventually or mainly because I was the daughter of a very feared man. Nobody except Jay and Gary had the nerve to make Dad angry. Even if Jay and Gary did try annoying Dad, something told me that they were trembling on the inside.

According to Mom, only Grandpa Jim had the skill to mold Dad. If Grandpa had been alive, he would most probably whack some sense in Dad's head and the divorce wouldn't have happened at all.

While sipping my coffee, I stared out of the café while cutting my pastry into tiny pieces. I rarely ate sweets thinking they'd add weight. I was extremely self-conscious after being scrutinized by everyone in my life. Both mom and dad exhausted me, especially since they were always bottled up. Since I couldn't find love, the least I could do was make my parents cherish the bond they had. So far, that dream seemed to flowing down the drain.

Sighing, I got up to ask for more tissues at the counter.

I heard the door open but didn't bother to see who it was. Once I had my tissues, I turned around and crashed into a suit-clad chest. The scent of cologne hit me like no other. It had literally whacked my senses and I forced myself to stare at the tall stranger.

"You alright there little lady?"

His voice was so thick and I immediately stepped back, bumping against the counter as I took in his handsome face. A chiseled jawline, a new scent of his aftershave, hollow cheeks, and icy blue eyes— I was greeted by a few of the most striking features I had ever seen in my life.

Little lady.

Fuck, I hated the way he called me that. Absolutely hated it.

"Done gawking?" He smirked and I flushed a bit.

"I'm sorry for bumping into you" I walked back to my seat. His words were still carved into my head.

Was I really that small...?

Not even Danny's called me that even though he was much taller than the stranger.

"This seat isn't taken is it?"

The stranger smiled and sat down next to me. All the warnings that Dad gave me flashed through my head. But I couldn't say anything because a part of me had been yearning for such a cliché moment. He looked about my age, handsome, rich, and cocky. He even had the guts to strike up a conversation with me— no stranger has done that before.

I wanted this to last.

Even though Dad might actually kill me, and the stranger.

"I'm Nicholas Shaw" His accent was different.

"You aren't from around here?"

"No, actually" He chuckled, "I flew all the way here from Canberra. My company's there, mostly my dad's. The flight landed a couple of hours back and now I'm here for some coffee while conversing with a pretty girl like yourself"

I couldn't stop blushing at his compliment. Nobody had ever flirtatiously admitted that I was beautiful before.

"I'm Lucy... It's nice to meet you, Mr.Shaw" I mustered a smile. Personally, I didn't say my family name since he might jump off his chair.

"Lucy" He grinned, "You're the prettiest little lady I've ever laid eyes on"

Multiple alarms went off in my head and my social awkwardness was beginning to kick in. The least I wanted to do was embarrass myself in front of such a handsome young man.

"Well," I got up nervously, "I kinda have to go to work. Bye"

When I dashed out of the café, it was already raining heavily. I hadn't thought of driving here since Xander Corp was a short walk from the café but now I had no umbrella.

Nicholas suddenly appeared behind me, "Can't go out in this weather, can you?"

"I'll call a cab" I replied.

He unlocked his car that was parked right next to us, "or I could drop you there? Wherever there is" He chuckled.

"It's fine Mr.Shaw-"

"Please, Lucy. Call me Nick" He smiled and it actually touched his eyes, "This is the least I can do for my first friend in the city. Besides, you work at Xander Corp, don't you?"

He pointed at the tag around my neck, "Yeah..."

"Great. I'm going there too. Get in," He smiled.

Reluctantly I got in next to him and in five minutes, we reached the company. We hadn't talked much— thank god— but he did ask about what I did and where I wanted to end up. Steadily climbing my way up promotions was the best answer that I could muster out of nervousness.

"And you, Nick? Who are you here to meet?"

"The CEO actually, I've heard a lot about him." Nick smiled, a sudden glint in his eyes, "Will you take me to his room, Lucy?"

I thought of it for a while, maybe he was an important businessman.

"Sure" I nodded and we went up to the top floor in the elevator.

"I've heard that he's quite harsh and blunt?"

"Maybe..." I gave him a weak smile, not willing to entertain the subject.

By the time we got out of the elevator, Dad's colleagues on the top floor greeted me to learn more about the stranger I was accompanying.

"He's a guest," I told them and hurriedly walked over to Dad's room. After knocking, I took a peek inside. Dad was on a call with someone but he gestured me to come in.

His eyes immediately turned cold on seeing the guy next to me. He hung up early and raised his brow at the young man.

"I'm Nicholas Shaw"

"Right. Mr.Shaw. It's good to meet you on such short notice. When was the flight?" Dad asked as I picked up his empty coffee mug and walked over to the machine.

"It was fine-"

"Eyes here young man," I heard Dad's irritated voice and turned to find a sheepish Nick.

I handed the cup of coffee to my father, "Thank you Cupcake. You can go back"

***

I figured that Dad didn't want me around the flirty Mr.Shaw any more than I did.

But in the back of my mind, I was convinced that Nick was stunning. Though without stubble, he looked like any college boy. While typing away at my laptop, I looked up on hearing the elevator ding. Nick had stepped out and was looking around - more like looking for someone.

My heart raced thinking he could be looking for me...

Was I really that special to a stranger?

I got up from my seat and walked over, it caused Nick's face to light up, "How come you never told me that your father happens to be the CEO? I would have tried harder to get into his good books" He chuckled

"I knew that you'd eventually find out..." I brushed a strand of hair behind my ears.

"Hmm, I just signed a deal with your Dad. It's related to the marketing of my business here. This means that I'll be seeing you more often, Lucy" He smiled in his classic smug way and caressed my face before pressing a kiss on my cheek.

"I'll be looking forward to it" He whispered before walking away.

I stood there frozen. Blushing like an idiot. Butterflies bungee jumping in my stomach as sweat rolled down my forehead.

Jesus, he was smooth.

***

When I went to meet Mom that day, I told her all about Nick.

"Calm down Lucy" She sighed while typing something on her phone, "He sounds like a playboy if you ask me, you should probably stay away from him"

"But... He's nice..." I mumbled while hugging the pillow.

The more I thought of him, the more butterflies I felt. He had a devilish smile and that made him all the more hot. He seemed like the perfect bad-boy and I couldn't help but feel drawn towards him.

Mom eyed me, "You're not falling for him in just one day are you?"

I felt a bit bolder this time. I'd do anything to defend my cliché fantasy, "You fell for Dad in one day"

"Yeah and now look at where we are" Mom muttered under her breath, "I still can't believe that someone actually clicked pictures..."

I rolled on my back, "Hmm... Dad was pretty mad"

"Of course he was. I ruined his reputation" She sighed.

"He was not mad about the pictures though, I think he was smug. But... He was mad about the title..."

She looked up from the laptop, "What?"

I smirked, "Goodnight"

"Lucy, what did your father say?" She nudged me.

"Aren't you curious to know?" I teased her.

"If you don't tell me what Leo said, I'll tell him about Nick"

"What!" My eyes widened.

"Surely you don't want that" Mom smirked.

"You can't do that! He'll kill Nick!"

Mom pondered over it for a while, "Maybe he will but I couldn't care less. Now, tell me"

"You're blackmailing me" I huffed and turned away.

She put her laptop aside and cuddled me from behind while rubbing her cheeks against my face. She used to do it all the time when I was in my teen years.

"Of course, I'm blackmailing you!" She chuckled, "But it's because I love you. I love you so so so much! You're my little rainbow cupcake and I can never stop loving you. You're so adorable-"

"Mom, stop" I giggled and pushed her away, "Dad was mad that they called you a stripper... Even though he's dealt with that scandal before. He asked Uncle Jeff to sue the reporters"

Mom's lips parted in surprise as she pulled away from me. Lost in her thoughts.

Dad always had this effect on her.

"Mom"

"Y-yes...?"

"Did something happen between you and Dad that... Um... Can't be fixed? I honestly don't understand it when he talks in codes"

"He told you that it can't be fixed?"

"Er... Kind of, yeah... Stuff that can't be forgotten. What happened back then, Mom?"

She sighed, "You're going to hate me"

"Of course not" I assured her

Mom stared at me for a while, "Let me finish up first" She mustered a weak smile.

I waited for a long time, two hours easily passed by. My curiosity was eating me alive but she was still on her tablet.

"So what ha-"

"I cheated on your father" She stated in a voice completely devoid of emotion. Mom didn't even look my way. She was too ashamed to do it.

"Wait... What?"

My entire world froze in seconds.

"I can't justify myself, Lucy. Your dad is the only one who knows... I... It's the worst thing I've ever done in my life.

I couldn't even say anything. I turned away, trying to process what I just heard. Never did I imagine my mother in such a position. She had always been my favorite person on the planet. I loved her so damn much.

She was my role model.

But now...

I was disgusted beyond words.

"Lucy I-"

"Not now, Mom... I'd like to sleep" I mumbled.

She didn't say anything more.

Lyrics: Catch Myself by WingtipLast Edited - 01/12/23

15: CLICHé

"And I should just tell you to leave 'cause I Know exactly where it leads, but I Watch us go 'round and 'round each time"

~-~-~

While typing away at my laptop, I heard a knock on my door. "Come in" I hummed.

"Mr.Xander, would you prefer having your lunch here or...?" Sonia asked.

"I'll be downstairs"

She nodded and closed the door behind her.

It was a relief that Kelly wasn't around. Lara had sent me her deepest apologies and I decided against taking aggravated action on Kelly, just for her sake.

Alvarez was the one who suggested that Sonia— his wife— had been looking for a job. She didn't mind staying the night since he could do the same, hence I was convinced to hire her.

She was far, far better than Kelly.

"Dad?" I heard Lucy's voice outside.

"You can come in, Cupcake"

She entered and closed the door behind her. Lucy was in a silky robe that was covering her bikini underneath. I wish she'd wear more covered ones but a part of me was relieved that she was only swimming at our home pool.

My baby had been very quiet all week and Danny even enquired if she was sick. But what surprised me was that my Cupcake hadn't met with Chelsea at all.

"You're not busy are you?"

"Just finishing up. What's wrong?"

Her face was slightly pale as she leaned back on the door while shuffling her feet, "Promise me that you won't get mad"

"Is it a boy?"

"What? No," She shook her head, "It's about Mom"

After that reckless one-night stand with Chelsea, we hadn't talked to each other. Hell, I hadn't even seen her. Now that my daughter brought her up, I was beginning to miss her again.

"What about your mom?" I sighed.

"Did... Did she really... Cheat?"

I stiffened.

"Who told you that?"

"She told me herself... That night when I slept at her place. Did you... Know?"

"Of course. She told me when you were a few months old"

"And you did nothing?" Lucy stared at me wide-eyed.

My headache was already building, "There's a scar on your mother's cheek. I caused that..."

She blinked a couple of times, "You- You're joking..."

I leaned back in my chair while loosening my tie.

"You hit her? What did you do to her?" Lucy looked furious.

"Cupcake... There's no excuse for what we have done to each other... It was all-" I searched for the right word "-Circumstances. But you came into our lives and you changed that"

She was about to head out of the door when I got up, "Don't leave, Lucy. Please. If you're going to hear about this, you're going to hear the whole part. I don't want you to misunderstand anything"

Lucy swallowed the lump in her throat and quietly sat down on the chair in front of me, "Thank you" I whispered and poured her a glass of tea.

"I never thought that I'd have to have this conversation one day. With you," I sighed, "But you deserve to know as much"

She nodded even though her gaze didn't meet my eyes.

"You already know that I didn't marry your mother because I loved her. Well, I was drowned in work all the time and your mom was... Well, she was... Uh... Young and beautiful, without a doubt. And I took advantage of her... With my wealth, I made her marry me."

Lucy glanced at me, "Go on"

"Right. I rarely came home on time, was drunk, mad, and... Uh... My youth got the better of me. Anyway, your mother was a couple of months pregnant while she um... became friends with her assigned driver... He used to take her to the hospital and all... His name was Trent," I sighed, "The first time I got... Violent... With your mother was when she was pestering me about something and I lost it. I'm sorry... I-"

"You should be apologizing to Mom" She mumbled.

I took another deep breath, "A couple of months after you were born, I found out that Chelsea cheated on me and I slapped her again. But she was terribly guilty about it... And at that point, we had no choice but to stay together because you were so young. Neither I nor your mom could pack up and leave you because of our problems..."

"So..." Lucy squirmed in her chair, "...You knew everything about each other. Practically hated each other. But you stayed married and put on all that romantic facade because of me...?"

"I don't hate your mother, Lucy. There's something that Jim told me once. No matter how insignificant it sounds, people do things for a reason. Your mom made that single mistake because I was, well, insufferable. And I used my past trauma as an excuse to treat her in the worst way possible. But we accepted that and moved on. Now, we don't have to pretend anymore so we're not together"

Lucy took another sip of her tea, "I'm gonna need a long time to recover from this"

Even though I refused to show it, her words made my heart crack. If I had a heart at all.

"I'm gonna go out and be back in the evening" She rose from her chair.

"Lucy," She stopped and turned to look at me. "Whatever I told you, it stays between you, me, and your mom, okay?"

She nodded.

"And Cupcake,"

She turned again, clearly annoyed.

"Please, don't hate us. You're the only thing we got"

"Stop saying that" I heard her grumble while heading out of my room.

[~ Lucy's POV ~]

"Two sandwiches," Nick told the food truck driver and after waiting a while, the man appeared with our meal. Nick even agreed to pay even though I was hesitant.

"Let's sit down over there" He looked over at the benches near the river.

He took off his sunglasses and stared at the beautiful view as we ate. "Are you feeling all better now?" He asked.

I smiled, "Yeah... Thanks for paying"

"It's the least I can do for you princess"

I flushed at the nickname that he gave me a few days back.

Nick had thought of temporarily settling in a villa nearby because Dad needed him in the company, he even had his own room at Xander Corp. Hence, he was always around and often brought me coffee and flowers. Even though we were just friends, he made it a point to flirt with me on a regular basis.

It had been just a week since I knew him but with every day, the butterflies inside me grew more restless.

Especially today while I was strolling through the streets to clear my head, Nick had popped up in his car and said that he was trying to go around the city but he was lost. In the end, our little city tour ended with him getting me sandwiches from a food truck near the river.

The spot was special to me since my parents had spent the night of their first anniversary on one of the benches. At least that was what Mom had told me.

Nick didn't know anything about my conversation with Dad but he had been bugging me to open up for a long time. The only time he gave up was when I admitted that I was hungry.

"I'll go get a coke. Want one?"

I shook my head. Just as Nick walked off, Danny began calling me. We hadn't talked much after I let him stay over. The memory made my heart clench.

"Hey Lucy" He greeted, "I was just wondering how you were"

"Hey... I'm fine..." I mumbled, wondering whether Dad had put him up to this.

"That's good to know. Are you at home?"

"No, I'm outside. Just going around the city"

Right then, Nick appeared with two cans of soft drinks, "I couldn't help but get one for you, princess" He chuckled while taking a seat next to me.

"Is that your friend?" Danny's voice suddenly went cold.

"Uh... Yeah. I have to hang up now"

"Do I know the guy?"

"No, Danny" I was losing my patience and Nick looked up, "Stop keeping tabs on me for Dad"

I hung up before he could defend himself.

"Boyfriend?" Nick raised a brow and I shook my head in horror.

"Childhood friend" I corrected.

"Ah. Where do we go next?" He glanced at his watch.

"Do you still want to hang around with... Me?"

He gave me a weird look, then leaned towards me, his hand slithered to my side of the bench and his face was suddenly close to mine.

"You're the only one I want to hang out with" He smiled.

I stared down at the coke clutched in my hands, my face was flaming. I jolted back feeling his hand skim over my cheek.

"W-what are you d-doing?"

Nick chuckled as he pushed a strand of hair behind my ear. It was the most romantic thing that anyone had ever done for me.

"You really are new to all this, aren't you, princess?"

"I- I..."

My heart nearly exploded at our proximity. I couldn't speak or move while being so absolutely lost in his eyes.

"Shhh" He brought his index finger down on my lips, "Let me treat you right from now, okay? Just leave yourself to me"

His words were so gentle, so comforting, and yet they felt so dangerous.

But I've wanted someone like him for so long.

Maybe I was falling for his charms.

I didn't have a clue.

Nicholas made me feel so overwhelmed that I couldn't do anything but nod dryly.

"That's my girl" He pressed a kiss on my forehead.

***

It was around seven in the evening when Nick parked his car outside the gates that led to my home. All evening, we had been driving around, stopping by bridges or parks, just walking around and eating. It felt extremely relaxing and I was beyond happy.

But whenever he fell quiet, he was watching me. These were the times that I was beyond nervous.

I didn't know what Nick was thinking about.

He always had this mysteriously smug face.

It scared me sometimes.

But I concluded that my fear was mainly because I had never spent so much alone time with any guy. It wasn't as bad as Mom or Dad had said. In fact, he was pretty sweet and too damn smooth. He would hold my hand as we walked and I often struggled to hide my blush.

He had called me Princess multiple times.

And I wanted to explode!

He was giving me the same quiet gaze now. Slowly, Nick moved his hand over mine, gently squeezing it.

"I'll see you tomorrow?" He smiled.

"Yeah..." I nodded and smiled back.

He held my hand tighter as I was about to get out the car. I turned to look at him, his smile widened and he leaned in to hold my face.

My heart raced.

My body went numb.

He leaned in for a kiss.

Unconsciously, I pulled back.

He chuckled at this, "We'll go at your pace. Goodnight, princess"

"G-goodnight..." I exited the car immediately.

My heart was banging against my chest.

Only if I hadn't pulled back!

Lyrics: Style by Taylor SwiftLast Edited - 01/12/23

16: Fallen

"You know how scared I am of elevatorsNever trust it if it rises fastIt can't lastUh oh, I'm falling in love"

~.~.~

After the long day, I was about to hurry up the stairs to my room when Danny appeared at the top.

"Lucy... You're back?" He walked over to me.

"What are you doing here...?" I gulped, fearing that he might have come to tell on me.

"Gary's party is in a few days and he asked me to tell your parents personally since there's a match coming up" Danny inched towards me but I felt terribly small under his gaze since he was already on the last step.

I nervously moved back since his eyes turned dark again. But he only seemed to close the gap between us as he examined my face intently. It was getting hard to breathe since his deep brown eyes were indirectly interrogating me.

"Where were you?" He asked, his tone a bit too similar to Dad's.

"Out"

"Out where?"

"It's none of your business" I frowned at him.

"Were you safe?" He switched to a softer tone.

"Yeah, I apparently came back in one piece"

Danny caught the sarcasm in my voice but didn't sound too amused, "Who was the boy?"

The boy. He was a boy himself for asking all these stupid questions.

"I already have a Dad. I don't need you to play his role as well" I grumbled and walked past him to go upstairs till he grabbed my arm.

"Stop behaving like a child, Lucy"

Danny had never been mad at me. Let alone talk me down like this. Today had been extremely tiring and I didn't need his bullshit to top it off.

"Let go of me" I mumbled.

His eyes went soft as he retreated his hand. But his gaze didn't meet mine anymore. Instead, a look of disappointment etched his features.

"I had gone to meet your mother earlier, she asked me how you were. She misses you terribly, Lucy. You should go see her..." With that Danny left.

***

Two days before Gary's party, I was online shopping in my cubicle. Since I had completely forgotten about buying clothes, this was my last resort. As I scrolled past different dresses, my frustration was beginning to grow.

"What's my princess up to?" I turned to find Nick leaning against the doorframe. He walked over and leaned over me from behind.

"Trying to buy a dress" I smiled.

"Is it a party? Am I invited?"

I chuckled, "No silly, my friend is hosting it"

"Hmm, I could be your date?" He leaned over my shoulder, his voice literally sent shivers down my spine.

"Dad is going to be there and..." I trailed off, too distracted by him.

"Oh, screw your dad" He groaned.

I frowned at him. Dad might be crappy but I loved him and nobody had the right to talk that way except Mom and myself.

"Don't say that Nick"

He sighed, "I'm sorry. Won't say it again"

I just hummed and continued scrolling. Nick's hand was on my desk as he leaned closer to watch the clothes, "I think that one's nice. You'll look hot in it, Lucy. Buy it" He pointed at a smoky red, short, tight dress that exposed too much cleavage.

"Dad won't let me step outside the house..."

Nick took in a frustrated breath, "The black one below isn't too bad either"

That one was actually good and I liked it but I preferred something more bright. "I'll pick the yellow shade," I told him and he nodded in approval.

Before I knew it, Nick pressed a kiss against my ear and whispered, "I wish I could see you in it"

My senses were shutting off one by one as he continued to graze his nose right there.

He was so hot.

"Mr.Shaw?"

I nearly jumped in my chair upon hearing a familiar male voice. Jay was standing at the door, a cup of coffee in his hands as he narrowed his eyes on Nick.

"I thought you had multiple meetings? What are you doing here?"

Nick scoffed, "You are just a driver here. Don't question me" He glared back and walked towards Jay to take the cup of coffee from him. But Jay held it away with a chuckle.

"I don't work for you, boy. I work for the boss and you being around her has everything to do with me. Lucy's my kid as much as she's Mr.Xander's"

Nick walked off arrogantly.

"Your coffee, young lady" Jay muttered.

"Thanks..."

"So..." He crossed his arms and stood by my desk, "...Why was that douche all touchy with you? Do I need to know something, Lucy?"

"I sort of... like him..."

"Hmm. There's nothing wrong with that, but make sure you know he's arrogant as fuck. A spoiled brat, rolling around in his dad's money. At least that's what your father thinks of him"

Why wasn't I surprised at his remark?

Nobody ever liked it when I made decisions for myself. They always told me off.

"Well, personally, I think that boy's just acting his age but he sure is arrogant. Not as much as your dad though" Jay chuckled. This was his effort to lighten up the mood.

He was so much like mom.

I missed Mom.

"Are you dating him?"

"I don't think so... At least, not yet..."

"Ah" He smirked, "So there are plans in the future. Just make sure your parents know"

I stared at him horrified, "You want me to tell Dad...?"

"Well," He scratched his face, "Even though my speech before was cheesy as hell, he's still your dad. And why aren't you talking with Chelsea? She called me today and sounded pretty low. You do realize that she's whining over Mr.Xander right?" He chuckled, "She's gonna drown in depression if you don't talk to her as well"

I rolled my eyes, "They both are whining over each other"

"Even better" Jay laughed and checked his watch, "I've to go check on Mathew"

"Okay, see you later" I smiled.

"Don't do anything stupid with that boy, okay? Take care of yourself"

"I know, Jay" I sighed.

***

The hug lingered far longer than I expected. Mom was always too emotional when it came to me.

She had cried buckets at home while mumbling that she was sorry for everything. I told her about what Dad had said. She didn't have to feel so bad about herself. Even though it was a scar on her part, Dad had caused her scars too. As disturbing as it sounded, they were even now.

Mom didn't think so though, she cried and kissed my face countless times. We spent hours talking and it felt like a huge weight had been lifted off my chest when I told her about everything.

"I just want you to know that I love you"

"I know" I groaned. She might have said the same thing a hundred times.

Mom beamed and hugged me once more, "Let's get you dressed for the party!" She rushed over to get my new dress. I laughed, she was always excited when it came to clothes. We got each other ready while laughing and playing along. It felt nice.

By the time we got to the resort, nearly everyone had arrived. On seeing Dad in the corner looking as dashing as always in a suit, Mom turned to me, "I'll go get you a cocktail"

I rolled my eyes. Alcohol was the first thing she thought of when it came to Dad, while he thought of smoking. They both were identical.

My friends came up to talk to me and I was surprised to find Arthur dressed in a suit since he always told me and Annie that a suit sucks every man of his freedom. He was always too dramatic.

When I was left alone, I randomly strolled the resort. Gary caught sight of me and called me over to meet his friends. He was laughing all the time with his arm possessively wrapped around Tania.

I was glad that he had found his person.

As I walked around more, I found beautiful quiet spots everywhere. I even found myself taking pictures, but that was when a text lit up my screen.

Nick: Seeing your dress in person makes me feel glad to have come :)

My eyes grew wide as I read and re-read the text.

Nick was at the party.

He was near me.

He had seen me in the dress we picked out together.

As started as I was, my jaw dropped when Nick sat beside me on the bench with a drink in his hands.

"What... What are you doing here?" I gasped.

"Tania was apparently my senior in high school and we ended up good friends. But I'm definitely surprised to see you here, princess" He smiled and I ended up telling him how my family knew Gary.

"Lucy! I was looking everywhere for you" Even Mom appeared out of nowhere and handed me a cocktail while eyeing Nick suspiciously.

"Nick, this is my mother"

"Ah, it's a pleasure meeting you, Mrs.Xander"

Mom flinched while shaking his hand, "It's just Chelsea" She replied, "I've heard a lot about you young man" She eyed the both of us.

"Good things, I hope" Nick grinned at us, "I happen to be a friend of Tania's so she invited me. I'm glad that I got to meet Lucy's parents as well"

"You met her father?" Mom stiffened.

"Well, I haven't talked to him since I got here but yes, we're quite fond of each other when it comes to work"

"Ah, work" She sipped her cocktail while chuckling.

"If I were you, I'd be careful before meeting him for anything other than work. Excuse me, there are a few other people I need to talk with" She smiled at us before walking away.

Gosh, I never imagined that Mom— out of everyone I knew— would be rude towards Nick. I didn't know why everyone was making such a big deal of me liking a guy.

"Your mom seems friendlier than your Dad" Nick chuckled.

"She's not always this rude..." I mumbled.

But what Mom had said wasn't wrong. Nick would definitely have to be careful when it came to Dad. I didn't know what he was capable of. Nobody knew what he was capable of. Unconsciously, I looked around for my father. He seemed to be somewhere in the lobby with Uncle Jeff.

Some of the couples were swaying to the warm music, and Nick suddenly hopped to his feet.

"Come on" He grabbed my hand, "Let's dance"

I stumbled as he pulled me towards the crowd. Before I could process anything, his arms were on my waist, while he put mine over his shoulder.

My fingers were cold and trembling, especially because of the eyes watching us. I was beyond nervous.

"Relax" Nick chuckled against my ear.

I stared at his blue eyes, they had a wicked glow in them.

The butterflies in my stomach had certainly caused a hurricane of emotions.

Gosh, I might have actually fallen for him.

Lyrics: Labyrinth by Taylor SwiftLast Edited - 01/12/23

17: Boyfriend

"I need a romance, one chanceI just wanna know, will you slow dance?I wanna slow dance if you're feeling me now"

~-~-~

"Are you seeing this...?" Arthur gasped while nudging his mother.

"Chelsea is that..."

"Yeah," I gulped.

My baby was there, in the middle of the crowd, swaying with the handsome boy in a suit. Jay and Annie were quick to march towards me, "Who is that?" Annie asked.

"Nicholas Shaw" Jay replied grimly, "He recently moved here from Australia and has spiked Lucy's interest. Right now, he's working with Mr.Xander as a partner"

Jay (being the best friend that he was) had told me everything that he saw in Lucy's cubicle. And from what I observed, the boy seemed used to getting what he wanted.

Maybe we were all overacting.

Maybe Lucy just needed her desperate phase to woman up.

But the way that guy grinned or the way his hands played with her exposed skin.

Fuck, it made my blood boil.

I could only imagine my fury as an ounce compared to Leo's reaction. He was going to lose his mind and I realized it better than everyone because I had seen firsthand, the way he raised our daughter.

Even when it was Arthur or Gary or even Danny, he felt uncomfortable if she was out of his sight for a minute. Only I knew about his tantrums.

"Shit"

I tore my eyes away from Lucy and stared in the direction Jay was gaping at.

Leo had stepped out of the hotel, his eyes widening at the mere sight of his daughter dancing with a stranger. Jeffrey saw it too and he immediately held Leo in place while squeezing his shoulder.

I tried darting towards the men. If he acted violently with Nicholas, everybody's reputation was at stake here. Poor Gary's party would be ruined. To my horror, Leo pushed Jeffrey's hand away and clenched his fists. In his eyes, I saw that he was preparing to punch the shit out of Nicholas.

I wouldn't have minded if we were alone.

But now...

He couldn't make a scene.

To my relief, Danny took action quicker than me. He blocked Leo and whispered something. Leo's insane expression faded by an inch as Danny led him towards the bar, his back turned against Lucy.

I honestly felt sorry for him.

Gathering my courage, I followed them either way. I knew my skills when it came to getting him relaxed. Even now, I trusted myself.

"Hey," I smiled and Leo looked up, scowling in the worst way possible.

Fuck, I hadn't confronted him since the last time we had sex.

Talking to him suddenly felt like a bad idea.

But my pride wouldn't allow me to back off that easily.

"He's just a friend," I assured Leo and took a seat next to him.

Danny sighed while taking constant sips of whatever he was drinking. He hadn't looked away from the couple. In his eyes, I saw the same anxiety as Leo's.

"He's a fucking player. Look at the damn way he's touching her. Just because that boy's father is a diligent worker, I don't think he has to be excused... Make her stop, Chelsea..." His last words seemed like he was begging me but judging from the way he squeezed his glass, I feared that he might break the glass.

I got up in an attempt to catch Lucy's attention.

She immediately pulled away from Nicholas and said something in the boy's ear. They walked away somewhere far from the dance floor.

"Should I go after them...?" Danny turned to me right away.

I sighed, "Stay here. Let them talk..."

Leo's harsh stare was on me now, "I'm going to end this" He shot up from the chair, threatening to follow the kids. I stopped him, trying to push him back down on the chair.

"Hear me out!" I snapped at him.

"What?" He growled, "You clearly aren't as concerned about this situation as much as I am"

"Of course I am" I bit back, "But think about it, Leo. She's over twenty. She can make her own decisions. You can't keep controlling her like this! It's her life!"

"And let her ruin her future by letting that guy have his way with her? Fuck no!"

I looked around, a few eyes had turned to us.

"Leo... Please... I came here just to see Gary happy. All the people here are important to him. You have to calm down. Lucy's not stupid, I know, and I trust her. She'll do the right thing in the end. Please, for her sake, calm down"

Leo clenched his jaw and turned away. When Danny left us alone to talk with his brother, I ordered another cocktail for myself.

On looking around, I found Lucy and Nick being interrogated in the corner with Annie and her brother. Our daughter didn't dare to look our way, I believed that it was for the better.

But watching them made me uneasy especially since Nick's hand was tightly gripping hers. He looked smug and confident, while she was blushing too much.

Were they just friends even now?

After a while, Jeffrey came around and sat next to Leo, they both were drinking the same non-alcoholic soda. When Leo couldn't take it anymore, he began digging through his pockets for his pack of cigarettes. He muttered curses when he couldn't find them.

In the years that went by, most of his ways hadn't changed at all.

It was already odd that we were sitting so close.

More of our photos might get circulated on the internet by now.

I glanced at the miserable man next to me. Poor guy, the only fault that he did was to love his daughter more than anything in the world.

Now, someone else had appeared to threaten that love.

But from Lucy's point of view, she never had any luck with boys.

I vaguely remember the one time when she was in middle school, her teacher informed me of all the bullying that she faced. Lucy didn't even tell us anything. I really hated it when she kept her true emotions bottled up. When Leo heard about it, he was mad at her for not telling him anything. In the end, he ended up threatening the parents of those kids that he would make their lives a living hell.

Probably the chain of incidents that began at a young age drove everyone away from her.

Besides, I knew Lucy too well.

She was withdrawn. Very badly.

Maybe all fault was ours. Her entire life, she was raised like a princess even though Leo never spoiled her. At this age, being with such a handsome guy seemed to be her first taste of freedom.

She must have wanted it so much.

But being the protective son of a gun that Leo was, he found it hard to accept it.

Reluctantly, I felt the need to run my hand up and down his back. He didn't spare me a glance, I was too used to it now.

"Do you really think that I should just... Let this go...?" He mumbled.

"You need to give them a chance" I whispered back.

Right then, Lucy and Nick walked over to us. Her face was beyond tense as she squeezed Nick's hand tightly. All this while, Nick had been going around talking to all the people that Lucy knew.

Finally, they came to us.

Jeffrey gave a light pat on his shoulder as a sign to look up. Leo glanced over his shoulder and his eyes first fell on the tangled fingers of Lucy and Nick.

"Dad... I-" Lucy couldn't bring out her words when Leo slammed his glass on the counter.

"Water," He growled at the bartender.

"Mr.Xander, I'd like to talk to you" Nick stated quite boldly.

Realising that I should leave them alone, I rose from my chair just like Jeffrey but Leo's firm grip on my wrist proved otherwise.

"Stay," He looked into my eyes. No matter how ferocious he was on the outside, in the depth of his emerald orbs I saw that he was nothing more than a terrified father. I sat back down.

"Lucy insisted that I should talk to you" Nick straightened his tie, "So, I'd like to say that I'm planning on making things official with your daughter-"

Leo shot up from his barstool making Nick jerk back in fear. He didn't look at them. Instead, he swallowed the entire water and stormed out of the place.

Jeffrey tried talking to him but one death glare was enough for everyone to step out of his way.

I couldn't let him go like this.

I loved him too much to be ignorant.

"I should have known that Mr.Xander would take it hard... But please, ma'am, the only fault that I've done is to like Lucy. And it's very hard not to" Nick told me. His eyes were still playful. I glanced at Lucy who was silently holding back her tears. Of course, Leo had never gotten mad at her to this extent.

"Nick," I sighed, "You do realize that it's hard for everyone to digest this and you may consider that we're being overdramatic"

"Not at all, I completely understand how you guys must be feeling"

"Hmm... Just remember this young man," I chuckled dryly, "If you ever hurt her, Leo's wrath won't be the only thing coming your way"

"Noted" He smiled.

I walked towards Danny who had a dark cloud over his head, "Sweetheart, please make sure that Lucy drives home safe, okay?"

He nodded, "Okay... But what if she wants to go with him...?"

"It's too early for that" I rolled my eyes, "Text me if she does"

"Yes ma'am" He nodded while drowning another drink.

As I hurried towards the parking lot, I saw Leo leaning against my car while scrolling through his phone. He was too distracted to notice me beside him.

My heart ached when I saw what he was staring at— our old photos.

Specifically, the one where he had a toothless Lucy in his arms, all dressed up and ready for her first day of school. She was grinning brightly in her father's arms and his eyes were so fond as he stared at her. Even though I had asked her to stay still while taking the picture, she was too excited to pay attention. It was one of the best pictures that I had taken.

Those were definitely the good times.

"Leo?" I touched his arm.

He immediately flinched away and stuffed the phone in his coat.

"You need to drive me somewhere..." He mumbled.

"Sure get in" I unlocked the car. He got in the passenger seat next to the wheel without another word.

"Where are we going?" I asked while driving out of the parking lot.

He began giving directions, every curve and every slope made me realize that I knew the damn place. I lived there for god's sake. He could've just asked me to take him to the apartment.

Lyrics: Slow Dance by AJ MitchellLast Edited - 01/12/23

18: Years

"Don't take this the wrong way/I want you to be happy/But it's hard to watch you fall again/'Cause now I gotta play pretend"

~.~.~

"One more" I muttered.

"Dude, you've never drunk this much in your life. You of all people should know that killing your liver won't help with healing a broken heart-"

Frustrated, I snatched the bottle from Gary and filled the glass to the brim.

He sighed and put the bottle away, "I've been telling you to make a move since what? 22 years?"

"Shut up" I glared and walked over to the window. Lifting the covers, I took a peek outside to make sure that Lucy and Nick were still there. He was dragging her by the hand like a lost puppy.

Lucy was dating him.

Nicholas Shaw— handsome, smooth, charismatic, and bold. I was nothing compared to him.

"I think they're leaving" I mumbled on seeing them walk towards the parking lot.

It was raining outside but I didn't care. I hurried out of the damn room, down the stairs, and straight into the downpour. Jay offered to lend his umbrella but I didn't want it. I was too frustrated to care.

Lucy and Nick under a single umbrella in the parking lot. Of course, that scoundrel was romantic. They stood next to his car as he began telling her something. I could imagine all kinds of flirtatious sentences rolling off his tongue since Lucy's eyes were wide.

The next thing I knew, he was smiling at her as his hand fondled her face.

My whole body wanted to spring into action and strangle him to death.

I felt my heart drop and shatter when he leaned in.

Their lips met.

And it wasn't even a chaste kiss.

Nick held her waist while pulling her towards him. He devoured her mouth.

My subconscious reminded me that I was in no place to judge, I had taken advantage of her naivety in the same way when she was underaged. At least, she was old enough now... But it didn't change the fact that she was naive.

Nick seemed to be having the time of his life because kissing Lucy tasted exactly like sipping nectar off a flower. I gulped, I could only imagine how it must feel now.

When they pulled back, she was panting. He planted one last kiss on her nose before climbing into his car and driving off. Lucy was so overwhelmed that the umbrella fell from her hands. She stared at the sky as though she was searching for something.

I went towards her and picked up the umbrella before holding it over her head, "You'll catch a cold, Lucy"

She sighed and walked over to her car. I followed her promptly like a valet and held the umbrella for her till she was safely inside the car.

"Danny" She finally turned to me.

I could listen to her say my name for a thousand years without getting bored.

"Yeah?" I gave her a pained smile.

"Do you think this is a bad idea?" She mumbled, "Nick and me"

It was a fucking terrible idea.

And I would definitely crush his damn skull if he ever hurts a hair on her head.

If he did something to make her cry, I would reign hell on him.

I was burning in the flames of jealousy, but I certainly didn't want to trouble her by complaining about how painful it was.

"Everyone just wants you to be safe and happy"

Lucy frowned and stared back at the steering wheel, "You know, you're starting to sound more like dad with every passing day" She drove off.

I squeezed the umbrella handle.

What the fuck was I supposed to say?

"Don't be with him 'cause I'll treat you a million times better because my entire heart belongs to you and it always has, since the first time I laid eyes on you... I love you, Lucy"

Sadly, only the rain heard me mumble.

I took out my phone and texted her saying that she should text me back on reaching home. Maybe I did sound a lot like Mr.Xander. But it was better than revealing my pathetic self.

[~ Chelsea's POV ~]

While changing into my nightdress, Danny texted me saying that Lucy was home. Even Alvarez texted the same since I had always asked him to.

I glanced at Leo from the mirror, he hadn't blinked when I stripped completely to take a shower. Instead, he was at the same spot I left him, smoking by the edge of the bed.

After getting my hair dry, I turned to the dull man. He was completely focused staring at random things. I sighed as he quietly let me undress him bit by bit till he was left in his pants.

"Stand up or lay down," I told him and he fell back on the pillow. Of course, the cigarette never left his lips. I unbuckled him and tugged the pants off.

"Should I take off his royal highness's boxers too?" I gave him a seductive smile, hoping that he would be distracted from Lucy but Leo didn't reply. He wasn't the slightest bit amused. Now, he properly laid back on the pillow and tossed his cig into the dustbin. I propped myself on my elbow while tracing my fingers over his chest.

"She's not going to love that boy more than she loves you" I assured him.

"But she loves him. An idiot that popped into her life just two weeks prior. And us?" He stared my way, "We raised her for 22 damn years"

"17. We got divorced" I reminded him.

"17, 22, 50, none of that matters! She is our daughter and no guy is going to take that away" He growled.

I took a deep breath, "Leo, you've never allowed her to date. You've never let her hang out with guys or even bring anyone home. Fine, even I wasn't too open to the idea. But-"

"I did that to protect her. The last thing I wanted was for her to end up with someone like me" He sounded more sincere this time but it pricked me to think that he thought so lowly of himself.

"You're not that bad..." I mumbled.

He glared at me, "You're the only person who thinks that. It makes no damn sense"

"Well, yeah, now blame me for loving an ass like yourself" I retorted and laid down on my side of the bed.

Leo exhaled deeply.

"Did I do something wrong?"

I glanced at him, "Huh?"

"With Lucy..." He mumbled, "Did I?"

Leo suddenly sounded like a child, unsure and confused about everything. His green eyes reflected anxiety and his heart was thumping too loudly now.

"Of course not"

I leaned in to hug his torso, I had missed the warmth of his body for a long time.

"You might have restricted her for a long time, but it was for her own good. She's bright Leo, and she's going to slowly build her way up till she reaches the highest position in your company. But since she's worked so hard, I think now's the right time to cut her some slack"

He didn't reply for a long time. I waited on his silence hoping that he would show some emotion, but nothing. Finally, I pulled away from him and turned off the lights.

Leo wrapped his arm around me when I climbed back in bed. He nuzzled into my neck with his eyes closed.

I smiled to myself, some things never change.

[~ Nick's POV ~]

Phone calls were annoying in the morning, especially when they were from Mathew. He was probably calling to remind me of the meeting that was in an hour. I didn't need him to tell me. Besides, I was already occupied at the moment.

"Babe...!" The girl squealed when I flipped her over. Her plump breasts were so good.

"Technically there's an hour left" I smirked at her.

"I thought you had your fun, baby" She giggled as I kissed her neck.

"Not yet. Got a long day today and I want to make every hour count" I mumbled while positioning myself at her entrance. The dirty blonde moaned as I thrust into her.

But the damn phone wouldn't be quiet.

On seeing Dad's number, I was even more annoyed.

"Nick, what the hell did you do?!" Dad growled but I wasn't paying attention.

"Right there, baby... Oh! Ah! Right there! Fuck!"

I chuckled at how loud she was.

"What the fuck are you doing?"

"What the fuck does it sounds like?" I grunted, thrusting as far as I could go. These sluts really knew their way around a dick.

"I'm ashamed of you" Dad's voice turned low, "But I'm even more ashamed of what you've set out to achieve. It's not going to work"

I slowed down and pulled out of the whore before draping the robe around me, "Don't you have anything else to tell me? I'm practically winning now!"

Dad sighed, "Leonardo's withdrawn his shares. He's terminated the contract and he emailed me a while ago. He's a professional man, Nick, but it's his daughter that you're playing with. I should have seen this coming"

"He did what?" I couldn't believe it.

It wasn't part of my plan. Why the hell would that old man withdraw the shares?

"I'll talk to him" I grumbled.

"You've done enough! The last thing I want is to bargain with Mr. Xander. Stop playing with that young girl's heart or I'll come there and end things myself"

"What are you talking about?" I scoffed, "Lucy trusts me so much and of course I love her!" Chuckling, I stretched out the word while picking a suit from my wardrobe.

"You're after his company and you know that marrying Lucy will easily put you in charge. I didn't raise you to be a fraud. Your mother wants you home, Nick"

I ignored his pleas.

"Most importantly," Dad sighed, "I'm concerned about your safety. Mr.Xander isn't a gentleman. He's feared by everyone for a reason and you're trying to take what is his... There will be extreme consequences if he finds out what you're after"

I rolled my eyes, "Lucy's going to be mine and so will that damn company. It's all your fault though, isn't it? Haven't you ridiculed me enough for twenty-five years? Am I not a brainless coward with a pretty face? You said it yourself. Let's see if I can conquer more than what you've done in a lifetime"

I hung up and threw the phone on the bed. The whore grew startled, "You alright there?" She asked.

Barely.

"Let's finish what we started" I smiled and climbed back into bed.

Lyrics: Play Pretend by Alex Sampson Last Edited - 01/12/23

19: PHOTOGRAPHS

"I always knew the day would come You'd stop crawling, start to run Beautiful as beautiful can be"

~.~.~

I glanced at the door.

He would storm in anytime now.

Just as I thought, Nick flung open the door and marched inside. He had absolutely no manners and now the bastard was glaring at me.

"Mr.Xander, withdrawing the contract was highly unprofessional on your part!"

What a boy.

I tilted my head, hoping to taunt him more.

Everything that Chelsea told me last night had been carved into my head. Sure, I couldn't keep Lucy forever. But that didn't mean that I would give her up to some kid without a fight.

If he wanted her, he'd have to deal with me first.

"I thought you didn't mix your work and professional life-"

"My daughter is my whole life" I gritted out.

He sighed and pressed the bridge of his nose, "Look, I get it. You don't think I deserve her and that's totally fine. It's just the beginning of things for us, Mr.Xander, and I promise to take care of her. To always keep her happy"

I fixed him with my cold gaze, "You'll need more than words to convince me, Mr.Shaw. And next time you decide to barge in without knocking, my security guards will escort you outside. Otherwise, I'll deal with you personally. Now, we don't want that do we?"

He clenched his fists as color rushed into his naked cheeks. He hadn't even grown completely. Pathetic.

"Is this a challenge of some sort?"

I glanced at him, then turned my attention to the laptop before me. Impatiently, he walked over and slammed his hand on my table.

"Don't you dare ignore me-!"

Shooting up from my chair, I clutched his shirt collar in my fist. He nearly stumbled back at our sudden proximity. Fear coursed through his young eyes.

I liked it.

"Get your skinny ass out of my office and never— I fucking swear— raise your goddamn voice at me" I pushed him.

His face was all red as he stormed out of my room without failing to slam the door shut. Arrogant asshole. Surely, Lucy could have done better. Almost an hour later, there was a faint knock on my door.

"Dad?"

I froze when Lucy popped her head inside.

While pretending to read something on the laptop, I ignored her even though it was hard. Never have I had to stay mad at Lucy for this long.

"Are you busy?"

"Can't you tell?" I retorted.

She closed the door and walked over to my desk. My little girl looked so pretty in her clothes today that I had to resist the urge to look up at her beautiful face and eyes.

"You won't talk to me...?" She whispered, disappointment clear in her voice as she stood behind my chair. Lucy sounded so broken and my heart was burning to hug her.

"Dad"

"Dad...?"

I swallowed the lump in my throat.

But I shivered all over when she wrapped her arms around my neck. Her tiny face was pressed against my stubble. It reminded me of all the times she'd hang from my neck like a monkey.

"Please talk to me, Dad... I don't like this..." Her voice cracked and from the corner of my eye, I saw that my baby was tearing up. "I'm sorry!" Her tear rolled down my neck and that stabbed my heart.

I immediately stood up from the chair and wrapped my arms around her. It didn't matter if it was a twenty-two-year-old Lucy or a three-month-old Lucy, I could never bear to see her cry.

"Shh... Cupcake... I'm not mad anymore..."

"Really?" She looked up with those big green eyes that I gave her.

"Yes," I smiled and hugged her again while kissing the top of her head.

She talked with me for a while and I was relieved that I didn't have to stay without talking to her. But it hurt when she said that she wasn't going to have lunch with me.

"Nick sounded pretty sad over something and I... I don't want to leave him alone... Dad, you understand right? I'm sorry about today but I'll make up for it tomorrow" She gave me a weak smile before heading out soon.

I was more sad than that fucker.

My phone buzzed in the evening and I was surprised to see Chelsea's name on the screen. I answered with a sigh, "Can't fuck today"

I heard her choking on something in the background, probably her coffee. She had the habit of drinking coffee during evenings and had engraved it in me as well.

"Now that you're done whining, you're just going to toss me away, aren't you?"

"Cut to the chase. I'm already pissed"

She chuckled, "Ah, must have talked to the boyfriend, huh? Lucy called me and said that you terminated his contract or something. I'm impressed"

"He needs to know that fighting me won't be that easy"

"Nobody's trying to fight you..." She mumbled and I could predict an eye roll.

"So, I called to talk about something else. Certainly, you've seen the news. Leonardo Xander and Chelsea Xander's fake divorce"

"Mathew told me. And?"

"And?" She scoffed, "Why are you letting them write crap like this!"

"I don't care about what they write. It doesn't affect me in any way" I mumbled while typing away at my laptop.

"Well, excuse me for pointing it out, but we are divorced"

"You didn't know?" Sarcasm was entangled in my tone.

"Haha. I thought I had to remind you since you seemed so cozy last night"

"You seemed cozier moaning my name two weeks back. What are we going to do about that?"

Chelsea went quiet.

"Wet already? Do I need to come over again-"

"Fuck you!"

She hung up leaving me annoyed. I texted Jeffrey again.

Have you located Trent yet? It's been a fucking long time since I asked you to do it ---

Jeffrey: Geez, no. I have a life outside your mysterious man hunts, you know. Like having dinner with my wife.

Do you have a lead on him or not? ---

Jeffrey: He's currently somewhere in Texas, I think. I don't know anything else.

Find his contact number or something. Fast. ---

Jeffrey: Shut up.

Don't text/call/fucking come over tonight.

Don't get yourself blocked, Mr.Xander :)

He was far worse than Chelsea.

***

It was around 8 pm and I found myself staring at the door wondering why Lucy hadn't shown up to say goodbye. She often left earlier than eight.

I walked out of my room and took the elevator to her floor. My subordinates greeted me as I walked past them. I made sure to nod and make them feel acknowledged like Jay had once asked me to. Before the freeze, I remembered not even glancing their way. Jeffrey's talk about karma had always haunted me and I wasn't taking chances again.

Lucy's cubicle was empty even though her laptop was on.

I had never taken the liberty of looking around her cubicle before, especially because I expected her to ask for a bigger room. She never brought it up though and I was quite surprised at how humble she had turned out to be. In a way, I was glad that she wasn't like me or Chelsea. It was for the better.

There were a couple of photo frames on her desk. The first one was a comical pose with Jay, Chuck, Chase, and Stuart. They had all been stubborn when it came to attending Lucy's first day in college. She was grinning brightly and I could see the twinkling of her eyes as well.

The next one was a selfie that I had taken when she was around 7. Chelsea was asleep in it while Lucy was snuggled in between us. She was biting her lower lips in an attempt to showcase the loss of her canines.

I still remember Chelsea being stark naked under the sheets but she was too exhausted to notice Lucy's presence. The night before had been long and sleepless as usual.

The third one was the exact picture that I had in my study. It was taken during a photo shoot where the interviewers wanted a professional picture of my family. Judging from her cropped brown hair, Lucy looked about four.

We were standing in front of the marble stairs that led to the glass doors of Xander Corp. My arm had been tightly curved around Chelsea's waist. Lucy was in her mother's arms while smiling at the camera. My cupcake looked adorable in her little dress that had orange flowers everywhere.

I sighed. Those were the best of times.

The last picture, however, was pushed behind the laptop but I inspected it closely.

It was a picture that Lucy had clicked of me and Chelsea. She had insisted on taking our photos that day, so I had to give in. To be honest, Chelsea and I rarely had any photos without Lucy in it.

My lips were grazing my ex-wife's ear as she glanced at me from over her shoulder. Chelsea looked as beautiful as always. I remembered whispering how badly I wanted to take her upstairs and bury myself inside her.

I was beginning to miss her all over again.

"Dad?" I turned to find Lucy next to the doorframe

"Why do you have this?" I mumbled and put the picture back.

Lucy sighed, "I like it a lot. That's why. Why are you here though?"

"You didn't come to my room and I thought you might have left without saying anything. Where were you?"

She bit her lip, "Uh... Nick's waiting outside. I said that I'd be going over to meet Arthur and Annie. He wants to come with me"

I clenched my jaw. Even though I had kicked that bastard out yesterday, he still had the audacity to hang around with Lucy at night.

"Will Danny be there?"

She scrunched her face, "Why would he be there?"

I sighed, "Make sure you're safe and text me every hour. Don't drink. Come home before 10. None of these rules are meant to be broken, alright?"

She nodded and kissed my face before grabbing her bag and leaving.

Only if she hadn't grown up at all.

Lyrics: Butterfly, Fly Away by Billy Ray CyrusLast Edited - 01/12/23

20: Tension

"Can I go where you go? Can we always be this close forever and ever? And ah, take me out, and take me home"

~.~.~

It had been three months since I began dating Nick.

And he was the nicest, funniest guy on the planet.

I knew that it could still be too early to acknowledge my feelings but I was falling badly for him.

After Dad had terminated the contract, he'd work for his dad's company from home. Once a month, he'd fly to Australia and stay there for a week.

I couldn't believe that I had survived a whole three months with a boyfriend.

When Dad had to go on a business trip to Italy, he completely left me in Mom's care. It was just so that I wouldn't stay over at Nick's place.

In fact, I had never been there.

He kept telling me that it was because my Dad didn't trust him yet. But when he does, Nick would wholeheartedly take me to his place and even Australia.

Sometimes I remembered all the warnings that I received when I was younger. People around me had made it so clear that boys would mainly want me for my body or money. Nick wanted neither of them and I was so happy.

Finally, I made the right decision on my own.

Even though Dad was still sour about everything, Mom wasn't like him. She had come to terms with the fact that Nick was my boyfriend.

The word always sent flutters through me.

Mom had once invited us over one time after tidying her room well. The paint buckets, stained clothes, and paintings were all put away neatly. She even cooked dinner for us which Nick appreciated very much. But, I soon figured that Mom was still cautious about Nick as she continuously kept asking him questions about his family and life in Australia.

The only thing that bothered me was that Nick appeared somewhat closed off. I talked to Annie about it and she advised that I should give him some time.

No relationship was perfect but I wanted ours to be.

Nick was too nice to lose.

In the mornings, he'd text me asking how I slept. Even though Dad had been mean towards him, Nick always asked how he was doing. Sometimes, Dad would insist on joining us for lunch. Even when he did, he stayed quiet or bickered with Nick. In the end, it was always Dad who won and he was very smug about it.

Nick would fuss over it all the time.

Sometimes I thought he fussed over everything.

The weather was too hot for him or his hair felt sticky or breakfast was tasteless... He found a way to complain over most natural things. I could only point that out as his bad trait.

Most importantly, Mom had warned me to leave him if he tried to physically or verbally assault me. It seemed like she was reminding me of her experience with Dad. But Nick had never once been mad at me. He never complained about things when it came to me. He hadn't even forced me into doing anything that I didn't want to.

When he stared at me sometimes, I thought I noticed something painful in his eyes. Like he was struggling to say something but he couldn't. If I tried saying something nice to lighten his mood, he'd smile at me, but the pain in his eyes would intensify.

I hated seeing him like that, or maybe I was just imagining things.

On the other hand, Dad's swearing and rules were slowly wearing off.

Even though he made it a point to always return home before 10, I was happy that he was getting used to Nick.

Maybe, it was because of Mom.

I thought that it was funny because even the paparazzi had grown tired of trying to decipher my parents' relationship.

Some nights, Dad would visit Mom. It was obvious to everyone that they found emotional and sexual (gross) gratification only with each other. Dad always appeared in higher spirits after meeting her. He had almost accepted the fact that his rainbow cupcake was seeing a guy.

It was utterly confusing but I refrained from interfering in their romantic drama. It could drive anybody insane, according to Jay.

Annie, Arthur, and Gary thought that Nick and I looked cute together.

But I didn't think that Danny thought the same. Of course, he would see things from my father's eyes. We rarely talked with each other anymore.

A few days after Gary's party, Danny had gone back to Illinois for work. He'd call my parents sometimes and they told me that he'd ask how I was. He was trying to be a damn guardian even though he was miles away.

I knew that I was mean to him the last time we talked, but I wasn't wrong.

Danny had been treating me like a kid ever since ever since I was a damn kid. Past tense. I wasn't a child anymore.

I was Nick's princess.

And it made me so proud.

***

My phone buzzed and it was Dad as I predicted, "This is the fifth time today" I groaned. Even Mom chuckled from beside me.

"Have you eaten, cupcake?" He asked.

"Yeah... All ready for bed now. Mom's been telling me about this new idea she's working on"

"Is she near you?" His reply was quick.

Mom shook her head at me, "Nope, she's still at the studio"

"What the hell is she doing there at 11 pm?"

Mom rolled her eyes and I giggled, "Dunno. She's busy you know"

"Whatever. Listen, Danny's going to be here tomorrow and he'll stay for two days. It's his friend's wedding. Gary said that he'll be busy so I want you to pick him up from the airport"

"Why me?" I groaned, "Can't you send Jay or someone"

"Jay's already slacking off beyond words and only you know where he lives"

"Fine" I mumbled.

"Thank you. I'll be back by the day after tomorrow"

"Okay goodnight Dad"

"Goodnight, I love you"

I chuckled, "Love from both of us!"

"What-"

I hung up as my mother stared at me with wide eyes.

"Shush, everyone knows it by now. Don't even try denying Mom" I pressed my finger on her lips with a grin.

"Sometimes I think that you really haven't grown up young lady" She rolled her eyes and plopped on the bed next to me.

"You haven't grown up too though" I snuggled into her arms.

"You love Dad just as much as the first day or even more. It's hilarious to watch him ignore you"

She groaned and turned away from me.

***

Nick was gently tapping on the steering wheel while I was on the phone with Danny.

"I can see you... Just keep walking straight" I mumbled.

Soon enough Danny spotted us and walked over.

"Hey, doc!" Nick grinned while getting out to help him with the bags.

Danny stared at him for a while, "Mr.Shaw, was it?"

"Please, call me Nick" He grinned and the men shook hands. "Lucy's family is just as much as my family" Nick looked over at me with those twinkling blue eyes that made my tummy flip.

Danny hummed while settling down in the back seat.

I glanced at him from the rearview mirror. His stubble had grown more roughly and his brown hair was messy from the long flight. He caught me staring and I immediately looked away, a faint blush crept into my face.

Stupid attractive doctor.

"I could have taken a cab home, actually. You didn't have to trouble yourself" Danny said in his thick yet soft voice.

"It's fine. Besides, I've been trying to get into the good books of the boss for a long time now" Nick chuckled.

I glanced at Danny again, he glanced back at me.

We had to stop making eye contact.

"You're here for a wedding?" I asked, sensing that it would be awkward not to talk.

"Yes. He's my friend from college. I'll be gone the same day as Mr.Xander returns from Italy. Going on business trips at his age must be tough for him"

"Yeah..." I sighed, "Since he's pretty close with the Italian partner, the project is important to him. He has to fly often. So, you'll be staying for just two days?"

Danny locked his eyes with mine again, "Yes. I prefer not staying here long" He replied curtly without looking away.

But I thought he liked his hometown...

The rest of the car ride, Nick initiated all conversations and they were mostly filled with all the little things that we had done together. Ranging from picnics, amusement park visits, and even boating.

"Lucy's always been a big fan of water" Danny smiled while staring out of the window. His brown eyes were twinkling from the sun, "Do you remember the time you jumped off a yacht? Just because you had floaties on?"

Nick laughed his head off while I turned into a bright shade of red.

Why the hell did Danny have to bring that up?

"Mr.Xander nearly had a heart attack 'cause you were just five or six. Even Gary was about to do the same after feeling inspired by you" He chuckled.

To my relief, the guys didn't bring up any more embarrassing incidents that included me but I was genuinely surprised that Danny remembered all the little things that we had done together as kids.

When Gary was an early teen, he was very fond of the cars, yachts, and money that Dad owned. He would always ask Dad to let him drive one of his cars for a day and Dad was fond of Gary at that time because someone had finally taken an interest in his collection of Cars and Yachts.

I remembered all the automobile-related conversations they had. The yacht trip was one such incident that Gary had been extremely excited about. It was very fun, especially since I got to swim around the pool with the boys and Dad.

Danny always took special care when I was in the water. If I ever found it hard to stay afloat, I remembered him hoisting me up in his arms.

The way he smiled hadn't changed over the years.

Neither did his character change.

Maybe I had been too rude...

***

"Lucy"

I turned to smile at Nick, "Yeah?"

Nick took both my hands in his and wrapped them around his waist.

"We're in broad daylight" I giggled.

"I know... But I don't want to see you go"

My heart melted at his words. His pale blue eyes were shimmering in the sun.

"I really want to take you to Australia" He whispered, "My parents will love you to pieces. Even more than they love me" Nick chuckled, "Come with me one day, okay princess?"

"Mm-hmm," I nodded.

He grinned and pressed a chaste kiss on my lips.

"The next one will be in the afternoon" He smirked.

"Such a charmer" I giggled while pulling away from him.

"Anything for my princess"

With multiple butterflies fluttering inside me, I hurried up the marble stairs and paused by the door to glance at Nick again. He smiled and blew me another kiss.

I loved how romantic he was.

Lyrics: Lover by Taylor SwiftLast Edited - 01/12/23

21: Leave

"Yeah, you can start over, you can run free
You can find other fish in the sea
You can pretend it's meant to be
But you can't stay away from me"

~-~-~

Nick had texted me saying that he would pick me up in an hour. I was excited to say the least. But there was a knock on my wall right then, and I looked up to find Danny beside Jay.

What was this about?

"There's something that I need to tell you," Danny mumbled. It was rare to see him wear a grim expression.

"Oh... Sit down" I beckoned to the chair next to me.

"You kids want any coffee?" Jay grinned at us and we shook our heads, "Coffee haters" He grumbled while walking away.

"So, what's wrong?" I glanced at Danny.

I tried to keep myself occupied with my laptop but it was proving to be difficult since he looked utterly stunning in a black suit and shirt.

He hesitated, "How... Er... How are you?"

"I'm fine. Everything's fine" I sighed, "You?"

"I'm not fine" His jaw tensed and his eyes turned sharp, "Nicholas isn't who you assume to be"

I froze.

"What...?"

"Yes, Lucy. He's a spoilt brat who's the only heir to his father's company. Nicholas Shaw is the kind of boy that you'll find in clubs surrounded by multiple women"

I stared at Danny for a while, my brows furrowed.

"What are you talking about?"

"Please, trust me. I've done my research" His eyes turned soft, almost pleading.

I stared back at the computer screen, "Maybe, that's what he did in the past. But it's not who he is today. You know nothing about him" My glare returned to Danny.

"Lucy, please, I... I even talked to the girl he invited to his place a couple of weeks back"

I gulped, "She might be his friend..."

"How damn naive can you be?!" He snapped.

Danny had never done this.

Never.

For a while, I felt scared.

His eyes were so dark.

"Don't you understand? They are not friends, Lucy. That bastard is cheating on you. Don't try defending him!"

A few moments of silence later, realisation settled on me.

"Did... Did Dad put you up to this?"

He stared at me in disbelief, "No Lucy. I did everything myself"

"You stalked my boyfriend?"

What the hell was he trying to pull?

"Lucy... I... I did it for your sake. He doesn't deserve you"

I stared at Danny's eyes.

They weren't the warm ones I remembered.

There was nothing warm about him anymore.

"Can you please go?" I whispered while looking away.

"Lucy... You still don't believe me? Ask him then. Has he talked about his past? About anything? As far as I know, nobody here seems to know much about him. He's clearly planning something, that will-"

I slapped him.

It was a weak slap.

Because my hands were trembling.

"Leave, Danny" I insisted.

He stared at me, disbelief etched all across his face. He looked hurt and mad. After giving me a cold stare, he got up and disappeared.

I didn't know if he was lying or telling the truth.

Nick's warm face popped into my head. The way he smiled, laughed, kissed, everything about him was so sweet.

He wouldn't cheat.

Of course not.

Would Danny lie for the sake of keeping me under his protection like an obsessive stalker?

Tears were rolling down my eyes before I realized it. I cried quietly into my desk.

Why did it overwhelm me so much?

Probably because I broke his heart.

Looking back, Danny had always been there for me.

Smiling, telling me good things, holding my hand, he did everything for me.

And now, I fucking slapped him.

I felt like shit.

***

"Hey princess" Nick grinned at me, his warm hands held me by the shoulders, till his face suddenly fell.

"Lucy, are you okay?"

My eyes were red and shrunken, it would be obvious to anyone that I had been crying.

I was not okay.

I didn't even know whom to trust anymore.

And I felt like screaming at everyone.

I wanted to dig a damn grave and bury myself in there.

"Hey, hey, shhh... Don't cry. I got you. It's okay" Nick enveloped me in his arms. He always felt so warm, so good.

He'd never cheat on me.

"Do you want to talk about it?"

"No" I replied while burying my face in his jacket.

"Okay, let's go to the river then. Get some fresh air and food, hm?"

I nodded and slowly pulled away from him.

***

Since I was feeling all gloomy, Nick suggested that we go get dinner the next day. He said that he had a surprise for me. After Nick dropped me off at the apartment, I was glad that Mom wasn't suspicious of anything.

The next day, it was busy as usual. Dad called a couple of times and promptly at 5, I went home. The guilt in my heart was still heavy. I thought that a pretty dress and makeup might help me but it didn't.

At 7 in the evening, I still had a sick feeling in the pit of my stomach.

My actions were crappy.

And I didn't know whom to talk with.

Arthur and Annie wouldn't have a clue on what to do.

Jay would tell Mom, who'd end up telling Dad.

And dad... Well, he was completely off the list.

Gary wasn't a bad choice but he loved Danny too much making him biased.

Only if I could directly ask Danny about what I was supposed to do.

I wanted to ask Nick.

But Danny's words had ignited a chain of self-doubt in me. I couldn't trust anyone at all.

An hour and a half had passed but Nick hadn't come to pick me up. I was already dressed in a red fluttery dress that fell till my mid-thighs. It was my shortest dress so far.

My phone buzzed with Nick's name and I answered the call.

"Princess... I... I'm so sorry. Something has come up at work and I need to attend to it urgently. I'm so sorry for ditching you, shit, I feel terrible"

"It's okay" I mumbled.

"Princess, I really am sorry. For everything..." He choked on his last words before hanging up.

I had no clue what he meant but I refused to care, my guilt was eating me alive. If I couldn't have dinner with Nick, I could at least break the ice with Danny.

***

I rang the doorbell.

Nobody answered.

I rang again to be greeted by silence.

Danny's front door had a peephole and the possibility of him purposefully ignoring me crossed my mind. He had every right to do so but I was going to be resolute too.

"I'll stay here till you let me in," I said.

The door flung open, startling me.

Danny stood bare. His hair was messier than usual, his stubble was rough and his eyes dark. Moreover, he was completely shirtless. His expression was quite obvious that he didn't care.

His eyes raked over me as he carelessly took a sip from the bottle of whiskey that was in his hand. Without a word, he marched back inside.

"Danny...?" I called but he didn't respond. He had soon disappeared into the comfort of his home.

I had made up my mind to come this far, but it was particularly difficult to muster enough courage to step inside. I took a deep breath and faced my fears, making sure to close the door behind me as I walked towards the lounge attached to the kitchen.

Danny didn't acknowledge my presence as he opened and closed his shelves while grumbling something. He seemed to be looking for another bottle to drown himself in.

"Danny we need to talk"

He didn't reply again but I watched as he wore kitchen gloves and opened the microwave to get something.

"I'm sorry, I shouldn't have done that. Please, at least look at me, Danny"

"Have you had dinner?" He muttered, without looking my way.

"No..."

"Sit down"

He pushed a plate onto the kitchen slab. I quietly walked over and sat down. The least I wanted was to make him even more mad.

The soup smelled amazing as he poured it into another bowl and placed it in front of me. He placed meatballs and spaghetti on the plate. "Thank you" I mumbled and began eating. He was such a wonderful chef.

"Do you like it?" Danny asked as he sat on the chair next to mine.

"Yeah" I smiled, "You cook really well"

He stared at my face for a while till he turned away again.

"Danny"

I placed my hand over his, "I'm sorry"

"Lucy, stop" He pulled away, immediately getting up from the chair, "You shouldn't be here"

"I'm not leaving till you talk" I pouted, "Hearing all that from you... I... I thought that you were making it all up so that I break up with Nick"

"It's not like you believe me either way though, huh?"

I stared at the plate with a flustered face.

"Figured as much" He muttered before taking a deep breath, "Finish your dinner. I'll drop you home after that"

"It's okay, I'll call a cab"

Danny glared at me, "I'm not okay with letting you go alone at night in a cab. Definitely not when you're wearing that" He pointed at my clothes with his bottle.

"You're drunk, Danny. It's dangerous"

He took an annoyed sip of his whiskey, "I'm still coming with you in the cab"

"Danny" I gritted my teeth, "This has to stop"

"What?" He raised a brow.

"You trying to be my babysitter. We are not kids anymore. I'm in my damn twenties. Stop being my dad's puppet"

He stared at me for a while.

"I respect your father more than anyone Lucy, and if you think that taking advice from him and obeying him is being his puppet," Danny scoffed, "Then you're just as young and stupid as you used to be"

I clenched my fists.

"I didn't come all this way to be humiliated by you. I'm sick and tired of this. Everybody in my life treats me as though I'm a glass doll. I can't go anywhere I like, can't do what I want to, or let alone, love someone!"

Danny narrowed his eyes on me, his lips twitching.

"What do you want me to do?"

He placed the bottle on the floor and turned to me.

"Stop treating me like a child. Like you're my Dad. You're far worse than him" Tears pricked my eyes.

"Be careful what you wish for, Lucy" Danny's voice turned husky all of a sudden. I shivered.

He had taken the same tone six years back before that fateful incident.

"It's the only thing I want" I managed to breathe confidently even though my heart was banging as his eyes kept growing dark.

"All my life I've been treated differently by people. It might be because of my father, but I hated it. My friends are the only ones who treat me a bit more normally. But you," I sucked a sharp breath, "You've been treating me the worst. Since the day I met you, I'm just a kid in your eyes. It feels terrible Danny"

He covered his face with his hand and turned away while groaning in frustration. "I can't take this anymore, I swear to god" He mumbled to himself before opening his eyes. His dark brown orbs fell on me.

"You want me to treat you like a woman?"

He stepped towards me, and I noticed how the ugly scent of alcohol coated his features.

I stepped back involuntarily.

"I— I..."

It felt weak to stutter but his proximity was killing me.

"If I stop treating you like a child, Lucy, then I won't hold back"

He dipped his head towards mine, his lips were now directly above my nose.

What was the worst that my father's puppet could possibly do?

Besides, knowing how Danny was, he'd continue holding back.

"You can't do it" I taunted at him.

But all life was drained from me when Danny dropped his lips to mine, devouring me without mercy.

Lyrics: Animals by Maroon 5Last Edited - 02/12/23

Merry Christmas hehe!

22: BLOOD

"Climb on board
We'll go slow and high tempo
Light and dark
Hold me hard and mellow"

~-~-~

"Danny!"

She clutched my shoulders and let out a terrified yelp when I picked her up by the waist. Lucy's face turned bright red from the kiss. It was just as hot as her sexy dress. I placed her securely on the kitchen slab and brushed her hair behind her ears.

"You asked for this, Lucy... And this... I've been dreading this the most" I mumbled while grazing my thumb over her lip.

"Danny... I..." Her green eyes were absolutely petrified now.

"Damn it Lucy, tell me to stop" I squeezed her waist, pulling her towards me.

Lucy was breathing heavily now.

"Just say it or I don't know what I might do"

My nose grazed hers, I could hear the erratic beating of her heart. Both our hearts. This had never felt so overwhelming before.

"Tell me and we'll go back to how it was. I'll stay away for as long as you want. I'll do whatever the fuck you want, please, tell me to stop"

The alcohol in my blood was eating me alive.

If I pushed her away now, we both might make it to morning in one piece.

Why the fuck wasn't she speaking?

"Wh-what do you want t-to do..."

My sunshine was so frightened that she was stuttering.

The most beautiful thing in the world was sitting before me.

In that damn red thing.

My sanity had died.

"I want to rip those clothes off your body, and I want to torment you until you say my name loud and clear— no, scream my damn name"

My lips were brushed against hers by now.

I didn't even know why I said that.

Fucking whiskey.

"I... I have a... Boyfriend"

Lucy turned her head slightly to avoid looking at me. Her warm, soft hands gently pushed at my chest. I even thought that they didn't want to move from there.

"Oh yeah? Why the hell won't you tell me to stop then?" I whispered while being drawn by the scent of her neck. Flawless as always.

Lucy bit down on her lower lip.

It killed the last of my brain cells.

"Fuck it"

I kissed her neck and sucked on her skin. I had been yearning to taste her for as long as I could remember.

"Lucy..." I whispered while trailing kisses and mild hickeys on her neck.

She let out a whimper when I sunk my teeth into her skin. My hands caressed her thighs as hers were around my neck, tangled in my hair. She shivered when I brushed my hands up her thighs till I got to touch the lace of her panties.

At a slow, agonizing pace, I traced my fingers all over her thighs and panties. I could easily feel the goosebumps I gave her.

Lucy squeezed her thighs together when I rubbed my two fingers over her sensitive entrance. She let out a little gasp, as though Lucy had never been given the pleasure to be aroused.

Had that asshole Nick had his way with her while only caring about himself?

"Relax sunshine" I whispered.

She spread her legs by an inch, "Good girl" I pressed another kiss on her neck.

Lucy clutched my shoulders when I rubbed a finger over her slit. Even her panties were starting to get soaked. I brought a hand up to hold the back of her neck as I slipped my fingers into the fine fabric.

"You're all damp for me, huh?" I whispered while running my fingers over her wetness.

My thumb pressed down on her clit and she leaned back further while clutching the other edge of the slab with her hands.

"D-Danny... Ah..." She heaved when I pushed a finger inside her.

So tight. So warm.

Her walls were already clenching around me.

"Ah!"

Lucy's eyes shot open when I pushed another finger inside and curled them.

"You like that?" I grazed the tip of my tongue over her clavicle.

She shivered and moaned louder when I thrust my fingers faster and harder.

"I... Y-ye- Ah... Ah!"

"Sunshine, say my name"

My thumb circled her sensitive bud.

"Do I make you feel good?" I kissed under her chin.

"Danny!"

She came all over my hand and fell back on the slab.

Lucy panted as though she had run a marathon. I licked my fingers clean without looking away from her.

"You taste better than I imagined"

Her eyes were wide and panic-stricken, "Wh-what...!" Before she could say anything, I clipped my fingers on her panties and pulled it off before stuffing it in the pocket of my sweatpants.

My erection was already begging to be set free.

"You look so beautiful like this, you know?" My breath fanned her core.

She threw her head back when my tongue flicked her folds. Her legs were over my shoulders and I pulled her by the waist for better range.

"Fuck... I could eat you for the rest of my life"

"Ah!"

She arched her back, nearly grinding into my mouth. I swallowed every drop of her and finally bit down on her bud.

Her fingers tugged at my hair, "Da-Danny...!" She whined.

Music to my ears.

"As much as I'd like to," I scooped her off the slab bridal style, "You'll bruise your back if we stay here"

Lucy panted in my arms while refusing to look my way. Her face had turned a dark red now.

"Look at me, sunshine"

My soft voice made her take a peek at my face, she suddenly grew aware of what we had done and buried her head in my shoulder.

Fuck, she was so damn cute.

"You really know how to drive a man insane" I rasped while pressing a kiss on her ear. She squirmed in my arms.

Lucy would be the end of me.

Dashing into my room, I placed her by the edge of the bed. Lucy turned away but she wasn't going to stop me.

My heart leapt thinking that she might change her mind if I waited longer. "I'm scared, Danny" She whispered. Her eyes were tightly shut.

For a minute, I almost forgot that Lucy wasn't used to any of this. A large part of me was glad. She stayed as innocent as I had hoped her to be. I sat behind her.

For her sake, I would slow down and show her a good time.

"Lucy..." I whispered, gently holding her shoulder, gently caressing my hand down her arms, before hugging her from behind.

"I've got you. Always have and always will. Don't be scared, sunshine. I'll be gentle"

I kissed her shoulder and peppered kisses down her back. She took a deep breath as I tossed her hair to the front and unzipped her dress all the way down. As a reassurance, I pressed kisses on every inch of her skin that I exposed. My hand found and unclasped her bra as well, letting it fall to her waist like her dress.

Pooled in her clothes, Lucy sat absolutely still.

I wrapped my hands around her waist while leaning over her shoulder. Her naked back was pressed against my beating chest.

"Your heart is beating so fast, Sunshine... Don't be scared. Let me make your toes curl, hm?"

Lucy turned her head to glance at me over her shoulder. I took that opportunity to hold her chin while letting our lips melt all over again. My hand slowly wrapped around her back and laid her on the bed.

Once I had pulled off all her clothes, I stared at the angel before me.

She turned away feeling extremely flustered. Lucy even attempted to cover her breasts and squeeze her thighs together to prevent my intense gaze from reaching them.

I grabbed her wrists and held them over her head while straddling her.

Lucy's neck, the bulge of her breasts, nipples, navel, thighs, and finally the sweet spot— I let my eyes run over every crook and crevice.

"I could worship you" I whispered and leaned over to kiss and savor her taste. My hands ran over her body, exploring, and getting her more aroused than she was. Everything felt so good.

"Danny..." She moaned when I squeezed her fairly small, yet adorable breasts. I took her hard nipples between my fingers.

"Fuck" I cursed and climbed out of bed, desperately searching my drawers for a condom. It had been a long time since I brought any woman here.

"What are you doing?" Lucy whispered while wrapping herself under the covers.

"I'm not going to risk your future" I grumbled.

The damn silver foil. Where the fuck was it?

"Danny... I'll take the pill..."

I blinked at her, "Why didn't you say it sooner?"

"Ah!" Lucy gasped when I pinned her down again. My erection clearly rubbed her stomach. In seconds I pulled down my sweatpants and finally set my member free that was leaking precum.

I had surprised myself, let alone Lucy.

She stared at me, scared to death.

"Trust me" I whispered and kissed her passionately.

Our tongues were in perfect harmony as I rubbed myself against her wet folds. Fuck, this was going to hurt her.

My tip pierced her entrance and she groaned into my mouth as I pushed it in.

"D-Danny..." She whimpered.

"It will be over soon, shh" I kissed the edge of her lips.

But I was only calm on the outside. Lucy was making me go crazy.

My hands wrapped around her waist and held the back of her neck.

"Danny! Ah!" She groaned as I pushed myself deeper.

"Fuck, Lucy, you're so tight..."

I completely pushed myself inside her and she arched her back, her nails digging into my spine as I slowly ground myself against her.

"You're doing so good, baby" I licked her ear.

Lucy's eyes rolled to the back of her head, "Danny... Oh god... Danny!"

Her moans echoed through my walls with every thrust. Inside and out. The pace was always greater than the last.

"I'm losing my damn mind" I confessed.

Sweat soaked our bodies, her hard nipples scratched my chest. They seemed like they could cut skin by now. Even my grip around her waist tightened.

"Does it feel good, sunshine?" I picked up my pace making her toes curl as she clung to me for dear life.

"Ah... A-ah...!" She had her eyes tightly shut.

"Is that a yes?" I went faster.

She groaned, "Ye... Yes... Hah..." Lucy was struggling to breathe now.

My face was right above hers as she mewled and moaned my name. Her hands were tightly wrapped around my neck as I rocked her body and the damn bed.

She made me crazy.

Insane.

I didn't know what.

"Hold on, sunshine, hold on..." I whispered while feeling my erection twitch inside her.

"DANNY!"

She yelled at the top of her voice as she came. I hit my release at the same time.

Our breathing was erratic and we were sweating terribly. But I felt fucking incredible.

I collapsed next to her and pulled her into my arms, her bosom was brushing against my chest as she fixed me with her exhausted gaze.

"Mr.Xander will most certainly murder me" I whispered while bumping my nose against hers.

Lucy chuckled.

The first real smile that she had given me in a while.

I chuckled back.

"Yeah, he will" She shook her head.

We stared at each other quietly for a long time. My hand was on her cheek again while gently brushing our lips together.

"Might as well make the best out of tonight"

I kissed her again.

***

A dark room.

So damn dark.

It felt like I was floating in the darkness.

I heard cries.

Soft, pleading sounds.

"Please! My boys they... They are just outside... Shark, not here...! Let's go upstairs... To the room... Please...!"

A loud whack.

My mother's soft sobbing sounds came again.

I was chasing her in the darkness.

But I saw them soon.

My mother was unconscious on the floor and Shark stood there with a broken rum bottle in his hand.

He turned to me, eyes wild like a devil's.

Before I knew it, his hands were squeezing my neck.

Shark lifted me off the ground.

I was shaking.

Crying.

Until suddenly he dipped me in a lake.

The water went into my lungs as he held me there.

His ugly teeth blurred over the surface.

"Piece of shit" I heard him mumble.

Till suddenly, he was punched in the face by a familiar big man.

Mr.Xander was there.

He wrapped his hands around me and lifted me out of the water.

"Breath, Danny. Breathe"

He kept repeating those three words over and over again.

I clung to him but I noticed that my hands were covered in blood.

So much blood.

***

I shot up in bed

My heart was beating erratically, I was panting, and sweating, and the images kept revolving vividly in my mind again. It almost felt like I was reliving the pain again.

Suddenly, I noticed the presence next to me.

Lucy was there, naked with hickeys sprinkled across her neck and bosom.

There was dried blood on the sheets.

I couldn't believe that Nick hadn't used her.

But I had.

Lyrics: PILLOWTALK by ZaynLast Edited - 02/12/23

23: Surprise

"Killing me slow, out the window I'm always waiting for you to be waiting below Devils roll the dice, angels roll their eyes What doesn't kill me makes me want you more"

~-~-~

The sound of my phone stirred me awake.

I winced as I tried to get up.

The events of last night suddenly turned into a whirlwind in my head.

Kissing, moaning, biting, and most importantly— having sex. Even though I wanted to be disciplined till the day I got married, I didn't know what came over me yesterday.

Maybe it was the undying thirst to want a man's touch or maybe I felt guilty for treating Danny like shit.

Whatever it was.

I regretted it every bit.

It looked like Danny did too.

He was tense as he paced up and down the room in his sweatpants, scratching the back of his head. Danny grew even more startled when he realized that I was wide awake.

"Lucy... I..." He gulped, making his Adam's apple bob, then stared around the room for words.

But all color drained from my face on seeing who had left the missed call.

Dad.

And nearly thirty other missed calls from Mom.

Even Annie texted me saying that she had told Mom that I was sleeping over at her place. She lied because she knew that I was having dinner with Nick.

I was so screwed.

Literally.

"Uh... Who was it...?" Danny asked.

Clutching the sheets around me, I sunk my head into the comfort of my knees.

I cheated on my first and probably last, boyfriend.

I ditched my parents.

And I slept with the guy I've known for years.

None of it was right.

"Sunshine..." He whispered as he slowly climbed into the bed and wrapped his arms around me. I remembered all the times Danny had called me that. It was painful to hear it again.

"It's Dad..." I mumbled, "He's returning today... I've to go pick him up..."

Danny visibly shivered upon mentioning my father. He even turned pale. The effect that my father had on everyone was absolutely mind-blowing.

But no matter what, he couldn't find out about this.

No one could.

No one must.

"I need to go home and change"

Danny sighed and cupped my face in his palms, "Lucy, we need to talk"

"Nothing happened. It will stay that way. Please..." I gritted out, my eyes pierced into his. If I tried to bring out any more words, I'd end up a soggy mess.

He stared at me for a while, the familiar broken look in his eyes had returned. It broke me.

"I'll wait downstairs" Danny pressed a quiet kiss on my head before closing the door behind him.

I tried staying brave while pulling my clothes back on. Nearly all the hickeys were in plain sight because of the stupid dress.

After taking a couple of deep breaths, I sneaked downstairs and found Danny pouring milk into two bowls of cereal. He could at least put on a shirt.

Secretly, I was hoping that he wouldn't notice if I slipped out of the front door.

But that was very dumb.

"Breakfast?" He asked without looking up.

"I have to go Danny" I didn't spare him a glance either before nearly running out the door.

***

"Ah, Lucy... Your mother called-"

I ran into the living room and up the stairs before Sonia could say anything more. I sincerely hoped that I hadn't given her a chance to notice the hickeys.

In the shower, I washed every inch of my skin multiple times. It felt as though I was trying to erase the damn marks he left. Every time I caught my reflection in the mirror, I looked thoroughly fucked.

By the time I got out and dressed in a full-sleeved turtleneck sweater, I was sure that Dad's flight would have arrived at the airport already. My clothes covered all hickeys fairly well, and so did the black baggy jeans.

To my horror, Danny had left his stupid hickeys on my jaw. I didn't even remember when or how that happened.

Damn him.

The concealer helped me cover all marks but it made me all the more late. Dad would either be extremely worried or mad or both.

"Where are you, Lucy? I've been waiting here for the past hour!" He said impatiently via the Bluetooth of my car.

"Five more minutes, I'll be there!" I hung up.

One by one, I had to clear the mess I created.

Even if it meant blatant lies.

I called Annie and she answered immediately, "Did you guys do it or not?" The smirk in her voice was quite obvious. My face was burning red.

"So you did huh" She chuckled.

I hated how she always analyzed my silence perfectly.

"Wh-what did you tell Mom...?"

"That we're having a sleepover but I don't think she believed me much... Anyway, she let it go when I kept insisting. You're going to have a long talk with her"

I was personally relieved that it was Mom and not Dad.

She'd at least try listening to me, unlike my father who would jump to conclusions.

Either way, I wasn't going to tell them or anyone the truth.

It was beyond embarrassing and wrong. So fucking wrong. They basically considered Danny as my bodyguard wherever I went.

Pretty ironic how that bodyguard was responsible for all the red marks on my damn body.

"You're such a good girl"

"Fuck, Sunshine, if you squeeze like that..."

"Lucy, you're so beautiful"

I was sweating from all the tummy-turning things that he had told me last night. He was drunk and wasted, but still, he made me feel good.

Physically, probably a bit too good. The more I thought of it, I felt dizzy.

Mentally, the guilty knots were building up with every passing second.

How could I look at Nick anymore?

***

"The jet lag is already taking a toll on me, and you had to be late" Dad grumbled as we walked up the stairs from the garage.

"I won't oversleep again... I'm sorry..." I sighed while leaning my head on his arm.

His warmth was something that I missed a lot.

"Have you been troubling your mother well?" Dad smiled down at me as we walked into the freshly cut lawn. It didn't take a genius to realize that Mom actually hadn't said anything to Dad. I was extremely grateful to her.

But I froze on seeing the familiar man on our couch.

"Danny?" Dad was just as surprised to see him.

"Mr.Xander" He smiled innocently.

"How come you're here this early?"

Danny's eyes momentarily fell on me and he licked his damn lips.

I felt like screaming now.

That mere gesture reminded me of all the things that tongue had done to me.

"I'm leaving for Illinois in the afternoon. I thought of seeing you before I go... Since uh..." He glanced at me, his eyes resting on my neck for a while, then my lips, and finally my eyes, "Since Lucy, told me that you were returning today"

"Hmm" Dad glanced at me, "Yet she overslept"

Danny faked a smile, the color drained from his face as he looked away from my father.

On realizing that I was going to blush and ruin everything, I excused myself by hurrying upstairs even though I thought of quietly hiding behind the staircase. I had to know what Danny was going to say.

"So," Dad asked, "When are you coming to be back?"

"Er... It's pretty unpredictable Mr.Xander. But I'll be a call away" Danny switched to his usual, warm tone.

"And when will your brother's wedding be?"

"Within a couple of months, definitely. You know how impatient he is"

Says the guy who was dying to touch me.

"Right. Fly safe" Dad told him.

With that, Danny left.

***

"Mom... I'm sorry. For the umpteenth time"

"I don't care about you being sorry, Lucy!" She snapped over the phone, "You still haven't stopped lying to me. It's your worst habit and you know how much I hate it!"

I gulped, no way in hell was I telling her.

If it was with Nick, I might have.

But now...

I had thrown that possibility out of the window.

Even if I was going to tell her, I'd only be comfortable after telling Nick and I had planned on confessing tonight since he invited me for dinner again. Danny was already on his flight back, there was no telling when I'd see him again and that relieved me abundantly. At least, there wouldn't be any more awkward conversations.

"Please Mom... I'll explain everything... Just... Just give me some time..."

"No matter what you do, Lucy, I'll find out" Her voice sounded grim, almost as though she was threatening me.

"And if your father hears about this... Well, I don't want to think of the headache he'll cause. That's why I'm keeping quiet right now. Promise me that you'll stay safe and sensible no matter what you do. There's something I always tell you, sweetheart, don't end up like me. Please..."

I rarely grabbed the exact meaning of her words. I always assumed that she was referring to her broken (yet passionate) relationship with dad.

Only if they'd come to terms with their feelings...

But now, I had to come to terms with my own feelings.

Nick didn't deserve a cheating slut like myself.

My heart broke into pieces thinking how he'd react but I had brought it upon myself.

Along with my growing self-hatred, I was beginning to hate Danny as well. He left me. Just like that. I was nothing but a body for him and it broke me so much.

All the radiance that he emitted, all the gentlemanly ways, the kindness... He ended everything just like that.

Or maybe I was still being too hard on him.

My mind was far too confused to process what I wanted myself.

Right now, Nick was my top priority.

I'd have to tell him tonight.

All the beautiful moments that he gifted me, everything would come to an end.

I didn't put much effort into my appearance. I didn't want to.

Deciding on a simple sweater and jeans, I headed out of my room. I had never given Nick an occasion to be mad, but tonight he'd want to destroy me.

I clutched my door handle, nearly on the brink of tears.

Why did I have to mess it up?

Why didn't I tell Danny to stop?

"Cupcake?" Dad popped his head out of his study, "Is everything alright?"

It seemed as though his pale green eyes had X-ray vision and had pierced into the depth of my soul— reading all that I had done and destroyed.

My lower lip quivered, "I-I'm fine..."

He immediately stepped towards me. His peppered hair was gelled well tonight, even his stubble was trimmed. Judging from his suit, it seemed as though he was about to go somewhere, but he took his time to caress the side of my face.

His eyes were examining me, concern laced all over his features, "Did that boy do something?" Dad's jaw clenched.

"No Dad!" I threw myself at him and hugged him as tightly as possible. His suit was so well-pressed that I didn't want to ruin it. I tried my best to hold in my tears even though a couple leaked though.

"I'm the worst..." I mumbled into his neck.

"What makes you think that?" Dad's soft voice was almost like a lullaby.

It made sense why I always fell asleep in his arms as a baby.

"I just... am... I'm so sorry..."

"Did something happen Lucy?"

Dad pulled back, a frown etched on his forehead as his thumb wiped my tears away. I wish I could tell him that I got carried away. He'd be so disappointed in me.

"No... I just... Feel sad, lately"

I hated lying so much, but I had no choice.

"Don't be, cupcake. Would you like to come with me? I'm going to Jeffrey's place. It'll be a bit boring, but we can have dinner there, catch up and all, you know. It'll be good" He smiled.

"Dad, I'd love to but..." I looked down, pulling away from his arms, "I am having dinner with Nick. He's waiting at the restaurant"

"What?" Dad growled, "You don't look too happy about it though, Lucy. Did he do something? I'm serious here. I'll break his neck"

I sighed, "He didn't... It's just me and my... well, mood swings"

"You're on your period?" Dad asked quite bluntly.

I scowled at him, "No..."

"Hah, good... I remember when your mother got those... I barely survived" He sighed.

I couldn't help but smile at this. "That's my girl, keep smiling like that, okay?" He kissed my temple and I nodded.

"Remember what I told you, be back before 10 or text me the address and I'll pick you up"

"Okay," I gave him another hug.

***

My head was throbbing by the time I reached the restaurant.

"You look beautiful as always, Lucy" Nick smiled and pecked my lips.

A tiny voice in my head said that somehow, Danny felt better.

I shut it down immediately.

Nick had pulled his chair right next to mine and it surprised me because he always preferred sitting in the opposite direction. I didn't question it but I sensed something was off since he seemed jittery.

I had hoped to tell him the news and leave as soon as I came before humiliating him after the food. Yet, the words always died in my mouth.

Nick ordered for the both of us and I told him I was fine with whatever he liked. The waiter brought the wine and I took a hasty sip to ease my nerves, and so did Nick.

We talked about random things for a while regarding his business in Australia and my dad's return. Nick was surprised as Dad let me go on a dinner date as he always hated the idea.

"There's something that I should tell you," Nick mumbled while staring at his plate of food.

He looked nervous and he was, as he began loosening his tie.

"Are you okay...?" I touched his arm, it might be the last time I get to do this.

He hummed and looked up at me with a smile.

"I need to tell you something too" I confessed. This would be the right time.

Nick chuckled, "Go on"

"No" I immediately replied, "You should go first" I bit my lip. My heart was pounding too fast.

Nick gulped then began digging through his coat pockets, till he took out a tiny grey box.

My brain instantly stopped processing things.

"Lucy, princess," He turned to me, his hand clearly sweaty, "I don't want to overwhelm you since you aren't used to these things... And I find that very cute..." He trailed off.

"I'm not perfect... I know, but after I met you, I'm constantly trying to be better every day. I'm so happy to have you, Lucy. No girl has ever made me feel butterflies before, it's only you. It's going to stay you because I find myself falling in love every time I look at your eyes" He grinned, then opened the box.

I nearly had a heart attack.

A bright diamond ring.

It was beautiful, no doubt.

"Will you marry me, princess?"

Bile rose in my throat.

I was disgusted with myself beyond words.

Nick didn't deserve to be broken this way.

Not after he had given such a sincere confession.

His blue eyes were twinkling excitedly like a young boy's.

"Oh, Nick..."

I found myself at a loss of words as I clutched his arm. "You don't know how badly I want to do this..."

"Then, say yes" He chuckled.

I stared at him, my throat dry, "I can't... N-not now... I'm sorry... I really am... Please, I don't want to lose you..."

There was a sudden disappointment in his eyes, he gave me a weak smile and put the box away before wrapping his arms around me.

"You don't have to give me an answer now, princess, but please don't keep me waiting for too long" Nick kissed my face.

Lyrics: Cruel Summer by Taylor SwiftLast Edited - 02/12/23

24: LUST

"Get on your kneesBeg me to stopI promise I'll love you if you do itSo do it for me"

~-~-~

Mathew was sorting out the files one by one on my desk while Jay was on the couch, leisurely drinking coffee.

"Sometimes, I wonder if I pay you just to operate the coffee machine"

Jay laughed in his classic cheerful way, earning a head shake from Mathew. "Imagine boss, if I wasn't here, this entire place would resemble a haunted house!"

"How do you even put up with him..." I grumbled, making Mathew sigh.

But he wasn't lying, Jay knew nearly everyone in my company. He had even proclaimed himself to be the 'work-therapist', by gossiping and dancing around without any work. Even though he mainly drove everyone around, he seemed to be spending more time in the lounges than actually working. My phone buzzed and I answered Danny's call.

"I was with a patient earlier, that's why I couldn't pick up, sir. How come you called?"

"Lucy's feeling a bit sick, I think. She said that she'd be on leave for a couple of days" I sighed.

"Hmm... Is her fever high?" He asked.

"I don't think it's a fever... She's skipping food according to Sonia and stays in her room for a long time"

"Did she eat anything unhealthy lately?"

I grunted, "That douchebag takes her out for food often."

"Oh... It could be food poisoning or just an upset stomach. It's nothing serious since she's not showing any other symptoms. If she's vomiting, I think you'll need to take her to the hospital. Do call me if the symptoms get worse"

"Right. I'll talk later"

"Have a good day, sir" He smiled as I hung up.

Both Mathew and Jay had paid close attention to our conversation as well. He got up from the couch and walked over to my desk, leaning over it next to Mathew, "I was wondering why she hadn't come in yet. It's nothing serious, right?"

"I don't know. She doesn't even tell me anything. It's all that boy's fault."

Jay smiled, "At this point, what will you do when they get married?"

My cold glare met him, "Get out of my office. Both of you."

Mathew's face fell, "But sir I-"

"Get the hell out!" I yelled.

Jay flinched and dragged Mathew outside with him.

My headache had returned. It always did when I thought about that damn Nicholas Shaw. I heard that he had proposed to Lucy as she told Chelsea and Jay about it, but was too terrified to approach me, her own father. When I found out from Chelsea, my first instinct was to grab my gun and shoot him dead. Until, of course, my ex-wife stopped my chain of thoughts.

The only thing that made me happy was that Lucy hadn't agreed yet.

It had been over a month since Nick's proposal though, maybe she was having second thoughts.

I was proud of her.

But that dickhead seemed adamant.

My day always turned out rough when I thought of my little girl wanting to spend the rest of her days with Nicholas. When I called Lucy in the afternoon, she hung up early and said that she was trying to sleep.

I sighed, she had never cared about me at all lately. Neither did she want to talk with Chelsea.

It was strange and something was not right. I'd have to get to the bottom of things, but visiting Chelsea was my top priority for now.

I would go over to meet her a couple of times a month since she seemed to be the only person who was guarded towards Nicholas. That boy had crept into Lucy's life, charming everyone she knew and loved, except us. Even though Chelsea had mixed feelings about him, she didn't trust him completely.

I didn't trust him at all.

At around seven pm, I texted Lucy that I'd be home late, then walked over to my car. Chelsea's studio was a small yet compact building north of her apartment. Young artists worked there, and professionals came there for recruits, inspiration, and to sponsor her. Even though we had divorced, a fraction of my company's shares were owned by Chelsea for her studio.

I walked past the revolving doors to reach the dimly lit corridor. At the end of which, Patty was typing away at the reception desk.

"Good evening. How may- Oh, Mr.Xander..." She looked up and gave me a nervous smile.

There were doors all around us and vases that decorated the corridor along with the maroon carpet. Stairs led upstairs to the more spacious rooms while an elevator waited behind the reception desk.

"Where is she?"

"She's in a meeting now, Mr.Xander. We are very busy-"

"Patty," I sucked a sharp breath, "Where is Chelsea?"

The woman before me gulped, "In the A/V room but-"

"Bring me a cup of coffee, the way Chelsea likes it." I walked towards the stairs before Patty could say anything more. She hurried after me, "But Mr.Xander, she is occupied! Chelsea's in the middle of a meeting with young artists from a university in Boston."

I paused and turned to glare at her. It wasn't the first time I was dealing with the nuisance on heels aka Patty. In fact, she resembled Mathew too much but I believed Chelsea gave her workers a lot more freedom, for obvious reasons. Patty understood the meaning behind my glare, hence she hurried back downstairs with a nod.

The A/V room wasn't unfamiliar to me even though I hadn't been inside before. Often, Chelsea was always in her own office and we'd talk there till I drove her home and fucked her. It was a no-strings-attached arrangement and Chelsea never complained, like always.

I opened the door and all eyes turned to me, including Chelsea whose lips parted in amusement. She was wearing a black pencil skirt and red blouse with her hair down. Beautiful.

"No visitors allowed." She crossed her arms and frowned at me.

The college students, boys, and girls, gaped at me. A few girls even took out their phones to take snaps. What the fuck was wrong with these kids?

"I'm not a visitor"

Calmly, I walked over to the long desk Chelsea was leaning against and sat down at the other end, facing the curious students. Chelsea had turned to glare at me for a while but sighed realizing that I wouldn't be leaving soon. She faced the students again and continued telling them things about art.

I noticed that the crowd of 19 to 20-year-olds had gotten restless ever since I sat down, watching them. Little did they know that I was interested in watching Chelsea's ass sway in that tight dress as she talked. When the email notifications on my phone went off, I took it out and began reading through them.

"Guys, I know that I'm not as interesting as the man behind me, but please pay attention," Chelsea chuckled, and so did a few of the kids.

"Who says you're not interesting?" I muttered at the screen without looking up.

A few of the idiotic guys in the back whistled at my comment, and a few made inhumane noises. Chelsea was silent and I was forced to look up, "What?" I snapped at her.

"Ahem, moving on..." She addressed the crowd again.

About half an hour later, I had taken off my coat and hung it on the chair next to me. Even Chelsea was done by now, and she smiled at the crowd confidently, "Any questions?"

"Are you guys still together?" A girl shouted from the middle of the crowd.

I was busy rolling up my sleeves and I ignored the kid completely. Chelsea on the other hand seemed extremely annoyed, "I'm going to refrain from answering questions from my personal life, young lady"

Other studious kids asked actual questions about art, and Patty came around then to slowly escort them to the other rooms and bring me coffee. The kids would be allowed to view paintings made by other artists until they got on their buses and left for good.

A few stayed back, discussing the paintings in the A/V room while others stayed to ask Chelsea questions. I had walked over to her side of the table by now and leaned back on the wood with my coat slung over my shoulder.

"Mr.Xander?"

A girl in a beanie and two of her friends came over to me, giggling. "I am a huge fan of yours!" She announced and held out her hand, "Carla" I ignored the hand and continued scrolling through my phone.

"You can call me any time" The girl in the beanie was now holding a chit with a wide grin. I was older than her damn father. The girl beside her spoke up, "Or all three of us-"

"Ladies"

Chelsea crossed her arms and raised a brow at the kids, "Patty's waiting for you outside. You should go and I'll take that, thank you very much" She snatched the chit off the girl's hand and sneered.

Disappointed, the girls went outside and now we were completely left alone. "It's all your fault" She grumbled, "You're sixty and you look like some hotshot Vogue model"

"58" I corrected.

"Whatever" She huffed, jealousy seething through her, "What are you doing here, Leo?"

"I'm pissed and I have a headache. You can make it better" I put my phone back inside.

"Well, Mr.Xander, I'm pissed as well. I can't just get on my knees whenever you want me to" She grumbled and walked out of the room.

"Chelsea-" I followed her down the hallway but she wouldn't stop till we were in her office. I closed the door behind me and leaned against the wall while she took the cloth off an incomplete canvas.

"Why isn't Lucy coming over these days?" She mumbled while working on the canvas with her brushes.

"I think she's sick... Or, I don't know"

"Sick?"Chelsea turned immediately, worry coursing through her, "Is she alright?"

I walked over and wrapped my arms around her waist before the back, "It's nothing serious"

"She didn't tell me anything..." Chelsea looked away, disappointed.

"Well, she doesn't tell me anything either now- stays in her room, Eats there, and doesn't come to work. I don't know what's wrong. Danny said that it could be an upset stomach 'cause she's not eating that well."

"Oh..." Chelsea sighed, turning back to her painting.

My hands hadn't left her yet, and I gently placed my chin on her shoulder as she painted.

"Chelsea?"

She hummed.

"Do you think Lucy will say yes to Nicholas?"

"I don't know, Leo... But if she does, we'll have to accept it"

My lips brushed against her skin, slowly leaving a trail of kisses.

"Are you sure that I can't kill him? It won't take too long..."

Chelsea rolled her eyes, "Don't be an idiot."

"Lucy's an idiot," I mumbled, "She's been an idiot ever since she met him"

"I was an idiot when I met you too."

"It's not the same!" I grunted and tightly wrapped my arms around her waist, pressing her back against my chest and sinking my teeth into her neck.

"Leo..." She whimpered, "Let me work-"

"Nobody's stopping you."

My hand coursed under her skirt and grazed over her warm core. Her grip on the brush tightened as I rubbed my fingers up and down the fabric. Chelsea tried to maintain her composure, but she'd lose it soon.

Without wasting much time, I bypassed her panties. "Ah!" She gasped at the sudden contact I made with her clit.

"Louder" I whispered and kissed the lobe of her ear.

"Those kids are right outside!" She exhaled and dropped her paintbrush as I tormented her.

"You don't expect me to turn suddenly self-conscious, do you?"

She chuckled at my words, "You haven't changed"

"You've not either. All you want is for those girls out there to hear that I'm in here fucking you and not them"

While sucking on her skin, a light moan escaped her again. My fingers prodded her moist folds. I pushed a digit inside her while circling my thumb around her clit.

"Leo..."

She brought her hand up to curve around my neck, forcing me to bite harder.

"Say my name again"

I flicked her insides and she clenched her walls around me.

"Leo!"

She groaned as I pushed another finger inside, curling them together.

"Fuck..." My breath fanned her neck as the erection kept growing in my pants.

My pace quickened, thrusting both fingers into her, making her moan louder and leaving scars on my neck.

"Aah!"

Chelsea stared at the ceiling, her knees shaking, breath labored, vision blurry. Her release coated my fingers just like always. I had my arms tightly around her to prevent Chelsea from losing her balance. She leaned back while breathing into my neck.

"Leo..." Her hand grazed my collar.

"Hmm?"

I stared at her brown orbs that were busy staring at my lips, her eyes flicked up to my own. Lust pooled her pupils.

"Bend me over"

I smiled.

Lyrics: Do It For Me by RosenfieldLast Edited - 02/12/23

Happy New Year <3

25: SICK

"Your mom's ring in your pocketMy picture in your walletYour heart was glass, I dropped itChampagne problems"

~-~-~

I sighed while taking another sip of water.

"She's gone to the store?"

"Yes. She left half an hour ago" Sonia replied, "Must have gone to buy medicines, Mr.Xander. I heard her throwing up"

I clenched my jaw, "I've to take her to the hospital then"

"For the whole day, she didn't even eat anything that I cooked" Alvarez sighed while plopping his arms on the kitchen table.

Right then, Lucy appeared outside the glass doors.

Her face turned sickly pale on seeing me.

She was wearing an oversized sweater and baggy pants that looked so out of place. Something was terribly long with her.

"Cupcake... Are you alright?" I wanted to hug her but she stepped back, almost afraid.

"What's wrong, Lucy?" I frowned, "I'm taking you to the hospital right away"

"No dad..." She gulped.

"Then stop acting so strange. What's that behind you?"

She was clutching something, "It's my medicines. I don't need to go to the hospital. I'm just tired and I'm not hungry"

Before I could ask anything, she hurried up the stairs.

"Lucy!"

She didn't stop. I heard her door bang shut.

"Did something else happen?" I turned to my workers furiously.

"No, Mr.Xander... She's stayed in her room the whole time..." Sonia gulped.

"Where's her dinner? I'll make her eat"

***

I knocked on Lucy's door for the hundredth time. Still, no response.

"Cupcake... I just want you to eat this. You don't have to go to the hospital. Just open the door so that I can see you"

Again she didn't reply.

I was beyond mad now.

Why the hell wasn't she opening the door?

It had been well over fifteen minutes since I began waiting and begging her to open the damn door.

"Lucy, like it or not, I'm coming in" I grumbled and used my spare key to open her door.

To my surprise, she wasn't on the bed. "Lucy?" I called again and saw that even the bathroom door was. After leaving the food on her bed, I knocked again.

"Lucy? There's dinner on the bed... Come on out and eat it"

I fucking hated it when she ignored me.

"If you don't start talking, I'm going to come in there" My lips twitched in annoyance.

"You asked for this"

I pushed open the door and found her standing next to the sink. Lucy was frozen, her eyes fixed on a stick in her hand.

My daughter was trembling.

And before I could process anything, her legs faltered and she collapsed on the floor.

"Lucy!" I yelled.

"Cupcake... Wake up... Please... Lucy..."

It felt as though a knife was constantly being stabbed in my chest. The pain was unbearable.

"Dad... I'm sorry..." She mumbled, half-conscious. Her head was on my thigh as I wrapped my arms around her body. I noticed the stick that had fallen next to her. I had seen the same thing with Chelsea.

It was on the day she found out that she was pregnant.

A heavy weight settled in my chest.

I didn't dare to take the stick.

Instead, I lifted Lucy and carried her to the bed. "My head is spinning..." She mumbled as I fixed her pillows. "It's going to be over soon... I promise..." I squeezed her hand and kissed it.

I took the phone in my hands and called the one person I could think of.

"I'm about to head to dinner with some friends-" She groaned.

"Listen... Chelsea... Please, come here... I- I don't know what to do..."

Never had I sounded so desperate in my life before. But as long as Lucy was involved, I didn't give a shit.

"What? Are you alright? Where's Lucy?" Her voice changed immediately. I was so glad that she understood the seriousness.

"Please... Just come home..."

"I'll be there" She hung up.

Lucy slowly drifted asleep and I watched her. Maybe I should have called a doctor instead, but I had to confirm something.

Something that I was fearing very badly.

In about half an hour, heels clicked up the stairs and Chelsea appeared near the door. "Alvarez heard you yelling... What happened?" Her eyes widened as they landed on Lucy on the bed.

"She fainted. In the bathroom" I clenched my fists.

"What?!" Chelsea sat by the bed, throwing her bag somewhere on the floor. "I-Is she okay... How... What happened, Leo?"

My eyes didn't leave Lucy. "There's something on the bathroom floor. I want you to take a look at it... I... I can't..."

Chelsea stared at me puzzled, then hurried to the bathroom and came out seconds later with the stick in her hand.

"She's pregnant"

I closed my eyes.

The nerve in my neck was twitching.

My fingers were trembling.

"I'm killing that motherfucker."

I shot up from the chair and marched towards the door. I would kill him. I would kill him over and over again. He was going to bleed, suffer, and die at my hands. I would punch his damn teeth in and break his backbone with my foot-

"Stop!"

Chelsea hugged me from behind in an attempt to drag me away from the stairs. As soon as we were out of the room, she closed the door behind us.

"Get your fucking hands off of me. I'm going!"

No matter how hard I tried to push her, she clung to me like ivy on a wall.

"I know you're upset. You have every right to be. Please, Leo, you have to calm down first. If you do something rash, that's going to affect Lucy. She's not healthy now!"

I clenched my fists so much that they turned white.

"Come with me" Chelsea now wrapped her arms around my fist and pulled me towards my room. She closed the door once we were inside and locked it. That wouldn't stop me from hunting Nicholas down.

But now, she was right.

I couldn't act on impulse.

No matter how much I wanted to crush his guts.

She made me sit on the bed and poured a glass of water from the jug nearby. The water calmed me down, but it didn't end my rage. Chelsea ran her hand up and down my back, while her head rested against my shoulder.

From the corner of my eye, I saw how panicked she was.

But she kept it all in.

"I'm going to call Nick" She whispered.

"Yeah, call him and I'll bury him here" I growled.

"No, Leo" She sighed, "You're not going to talk to him. You can't hurt him. Since he's the father of the child, he needs to know. But there are chances that the stick can go wrong... We'll have to take her to the hospital to make sure"

I scowled at her, "Lucy won't go that far... It must be wrong"

"We'll see, love, we'll see" She sighed.

"Call the fucker. Right now"

"Now?" She stared at me wide-eyed, "It's nearly 11"

"He doesn't need to sleep. Call him for fuck's sake"

She frowned back at me, "No Leo. He doesn't. But we do. I'm staying with Lucy tonight. She needs to eat and sleep, and so do you"

***

Chelsea was upstairs with Lucy and I was in the kitchen drowning nearly a gallon of water for the past hour.

I couldn't sleep. Not tonight.

My mind was too busy plotting all the brutal ways in which I could kill Nicholas.

"Leo..." Chelsea walked over to me. I rarely saw her look emotionally drained, "Lucy's awake and she's eating. But she's still not talking" Chelsea sighed.

I filled my glass with water and handed it to her, "Drink"

She gave me a small smile, "Thank you"

No matter how hard I tried, not even Chelsea being in my house was distracting me. The heavy weight in my chest hadn't died. It was growing with every second.

She hugged my face and pulled me towards her waist. A heavy sigh escaped me when she ran her fingers through my hair.

"She's asking about you"

"She's lucky that I haven't disowned her. Yet" I growled, immediately regretting my words.

"Shh... I know you don't mean that..." Chelsea whispered, "I'll call Nick in the morning. Okay? Don't hurt him"

"We'll see about that-"

She tilted my head up while forcing me to look into her eyes, "You're not hurting him, Leonardo"

"If they want to keep the baby, that's their decision. She's an adult, he's an adult. There's nothing we can do, okay? And I meant it when

I said no physical torture, no death glares, no verbal blackmailing, no nothing. Got it?"

"I'm going to bed" I grumbled and got up from the chair.

"Want me to kiss you goodnight?" She smiled.

I ignored her and headed to my room before locking the door.

***

My finger was impatiently tapping my thigh and my eyes never left the boy before my eyes. He squirmed uncomfortably on the couch while looking away nervously.

Chelsea appeared soon and sat down next to me, her hand patted mine as a warning.

But the more I stared at the fucker, the more I wanted to rip his intestines out. "Why are you guys scaring me like this?" Nick gave a dry laugh that was met with our silence and my intensified glare.

"Look, Nick... How do I say this... You're a responsible young man"

I snapped my head in Chelsea's direction, "He's the fucking opposite"

"Leo!" She glared back at me.

The boy eyed the both of us puzzled.

"Where's Lucy by the way?" He asked with that damn goofy grin.

Fuck, I had to hold it in.

"She's a bit... sick"

"Sick?" He frowned, "She didn't tell me. Can I see her?" He got up.

"Sit the fuck down" I clenched my fist.

Nick flinched and Chelsea palmed her face with a sigh. Obediently enough, Nick sat back down, his lips suddenly curved into a smile.

"Hold on, are you mad 'cause it's good news? 'cause she said yes?" His grin widened.

And I lost it.

I completely fucking lost it and landed a hook on his face.

Nick fell on the couch, he stared at me, eyes wide with fear and a bruise on his jaw. He raised his hand when I was about to launch another punch in his direction, but Chelsea pulled me back by my other hand.

"What the fuck?! Why the hell did you punch me!"

"Lucy's fucking pregnant!" I spat.

His jaw dropped.

"W-what...? H-how...?"

I shook Chelsea away and paced up and down the room, desperately trying to calm down.

"She did the test here, Nick. It was positive last night and she's been showing the symptoms for a few days..."

He gulped, "I need to talk to her"

"She's upstairs" Chelsea mumbled.

He gave me a cautious glance and ran up the stairs, wincing from the pain.

Chelsea walked over to me and took my fist in her hands, noting the mild bruise. "You have to stop this absurdity... Leo... It's all up to them now"

"You know what?" I growled at her, "I don't fucking give a shit anymore. Lucy's going to suffer with him and she doesn't see it. She's brought this upon herself and I'm not going to be involved at all. Let them fucking move in together, I don't care"

I pulled away from Chelsea and walked towards the garage, "Where are you going!"

"To hell!" I yelled.

www.ingramcontent.com/pod-product-compliance
Lightning Source LLC
Chambersburg PA
CBHW071220080526
44587CB00013BA/1442